This Book Belongs To:

MW00892229

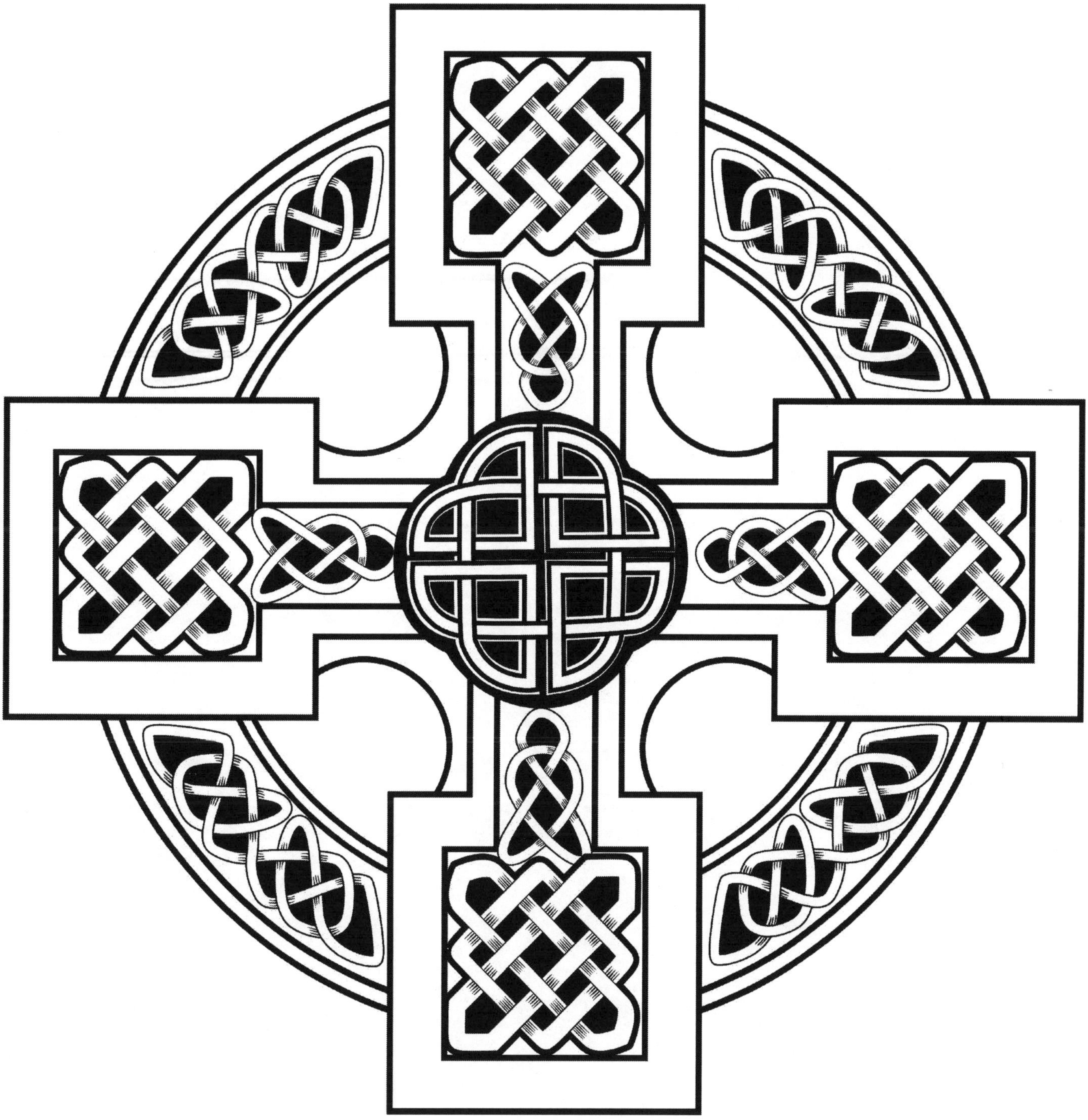

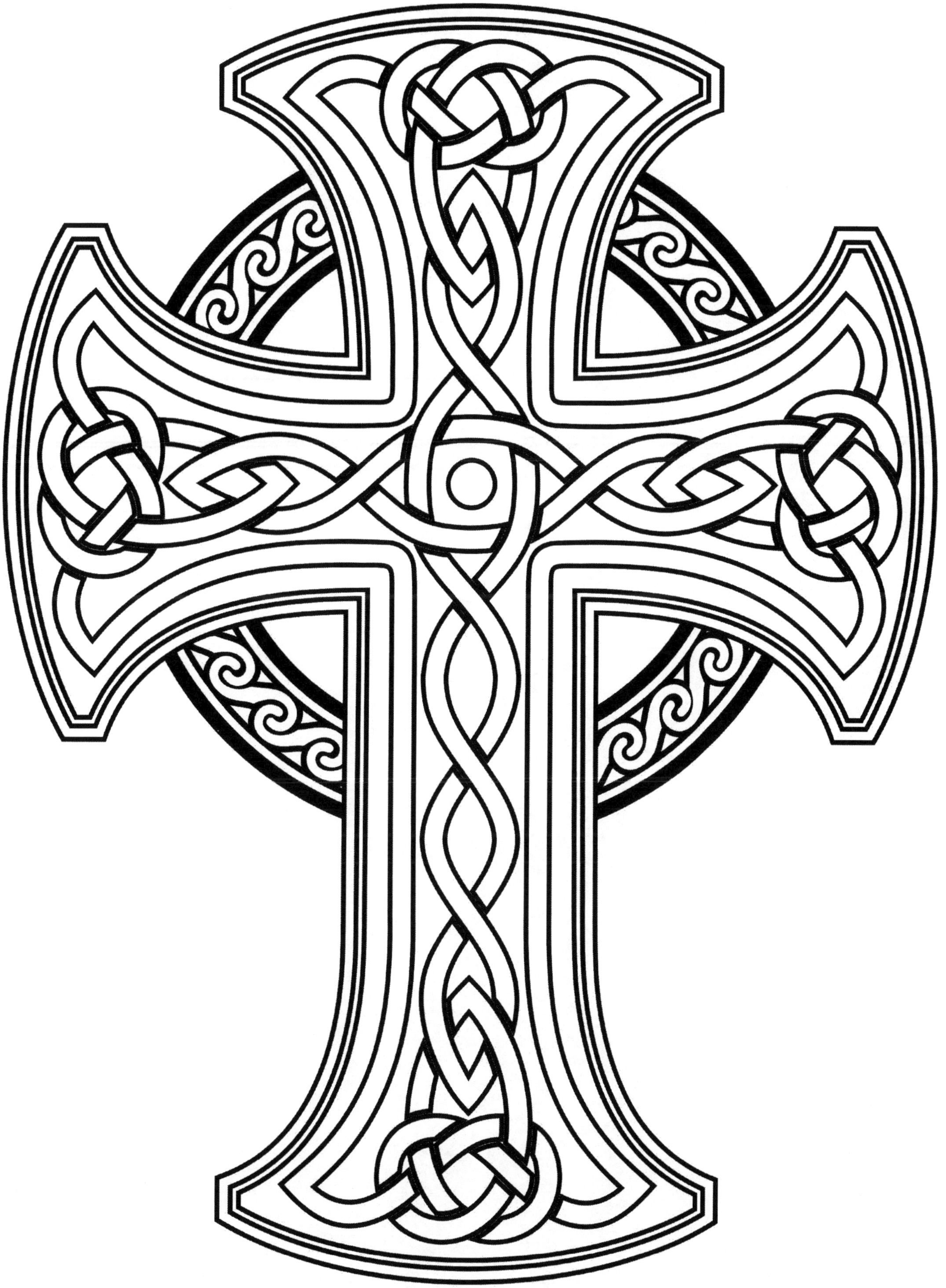

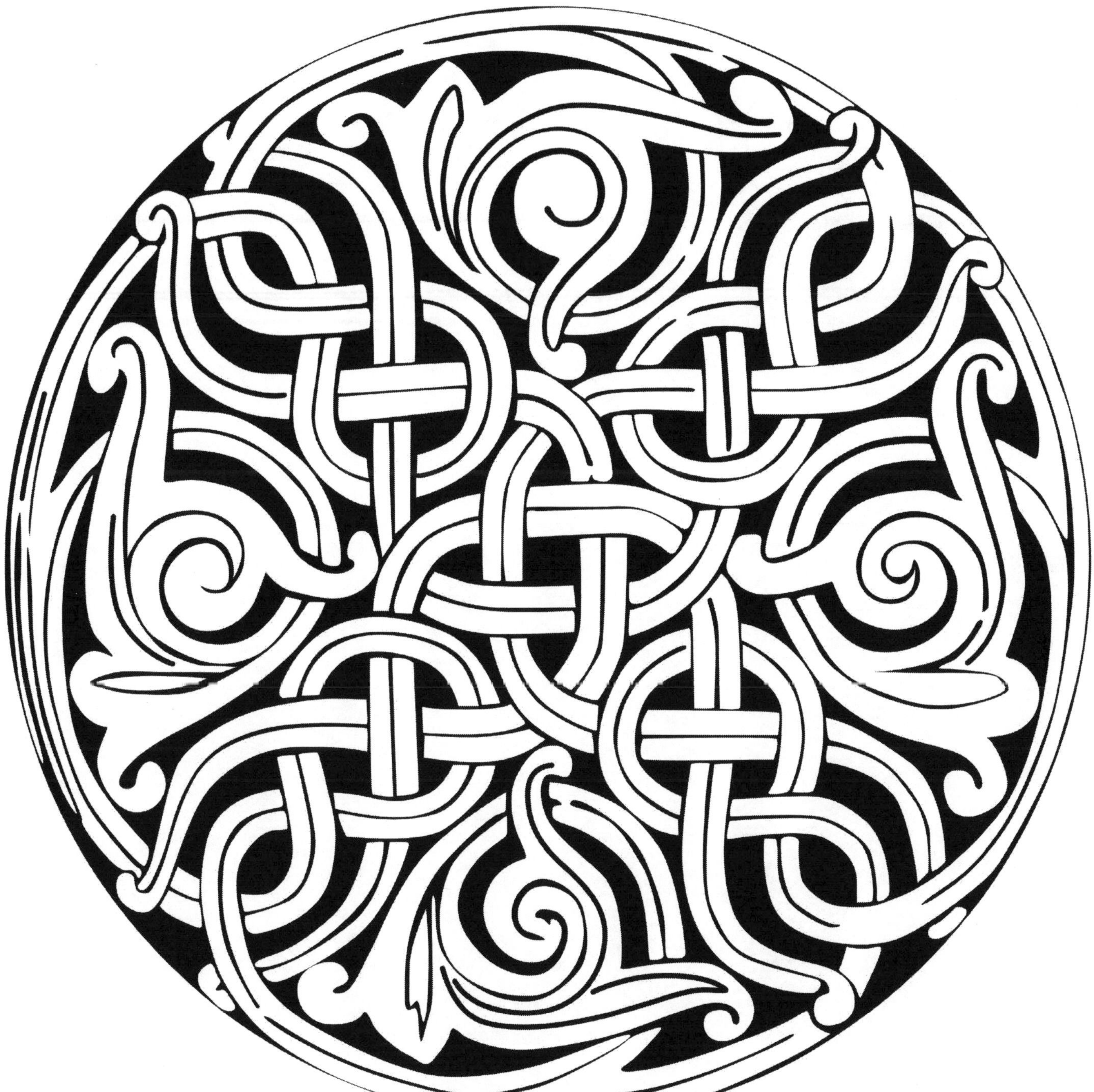

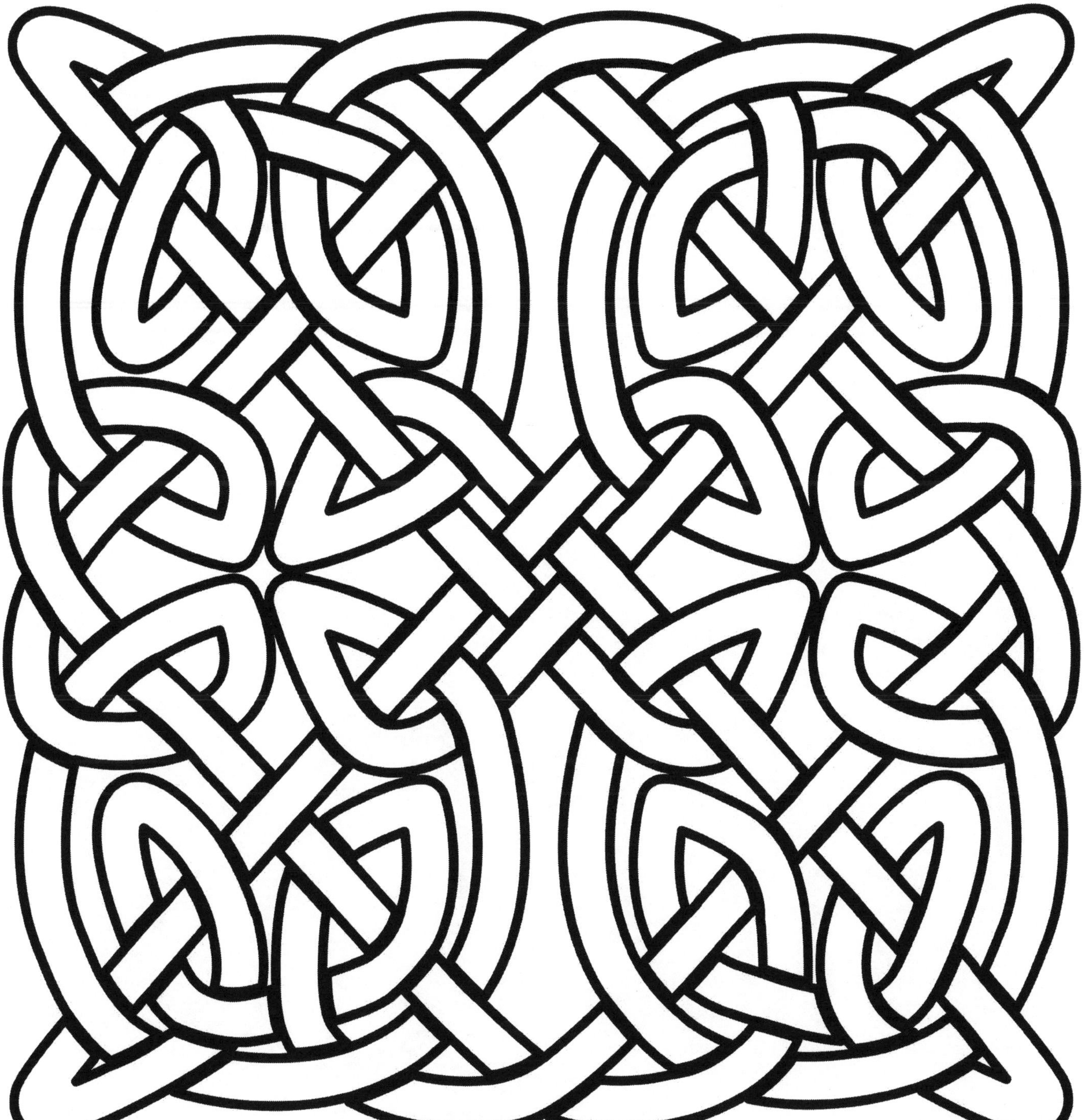

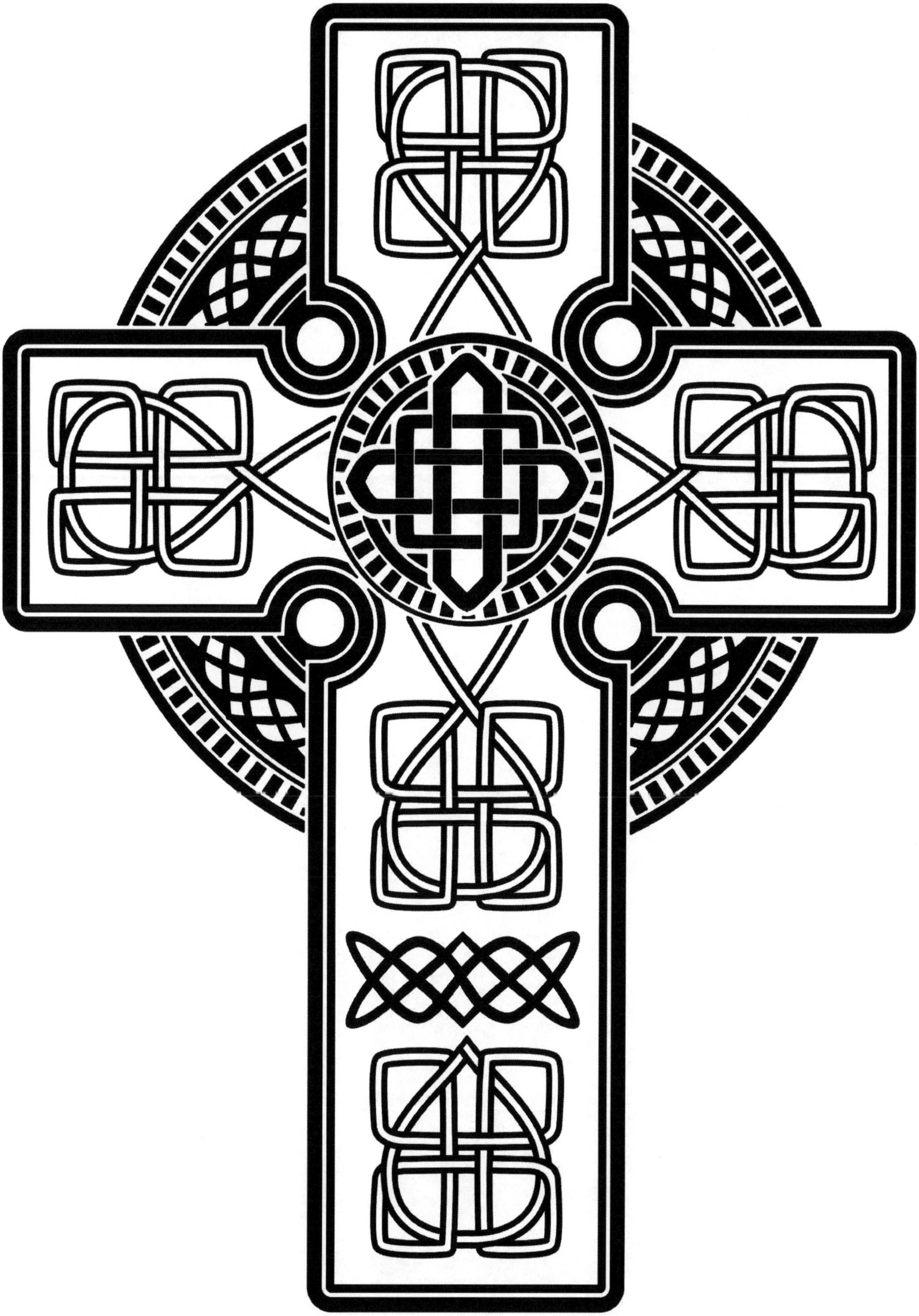

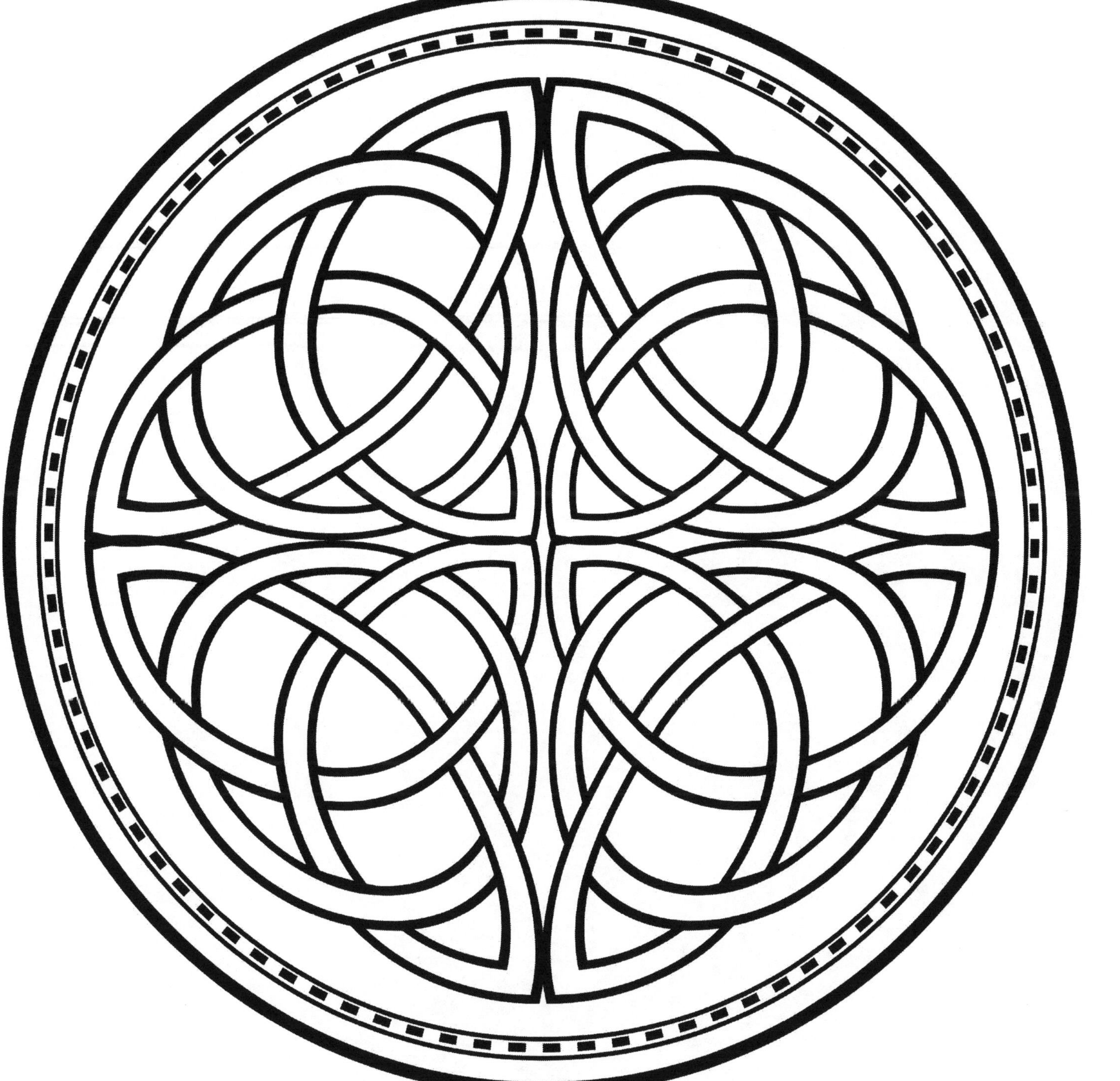

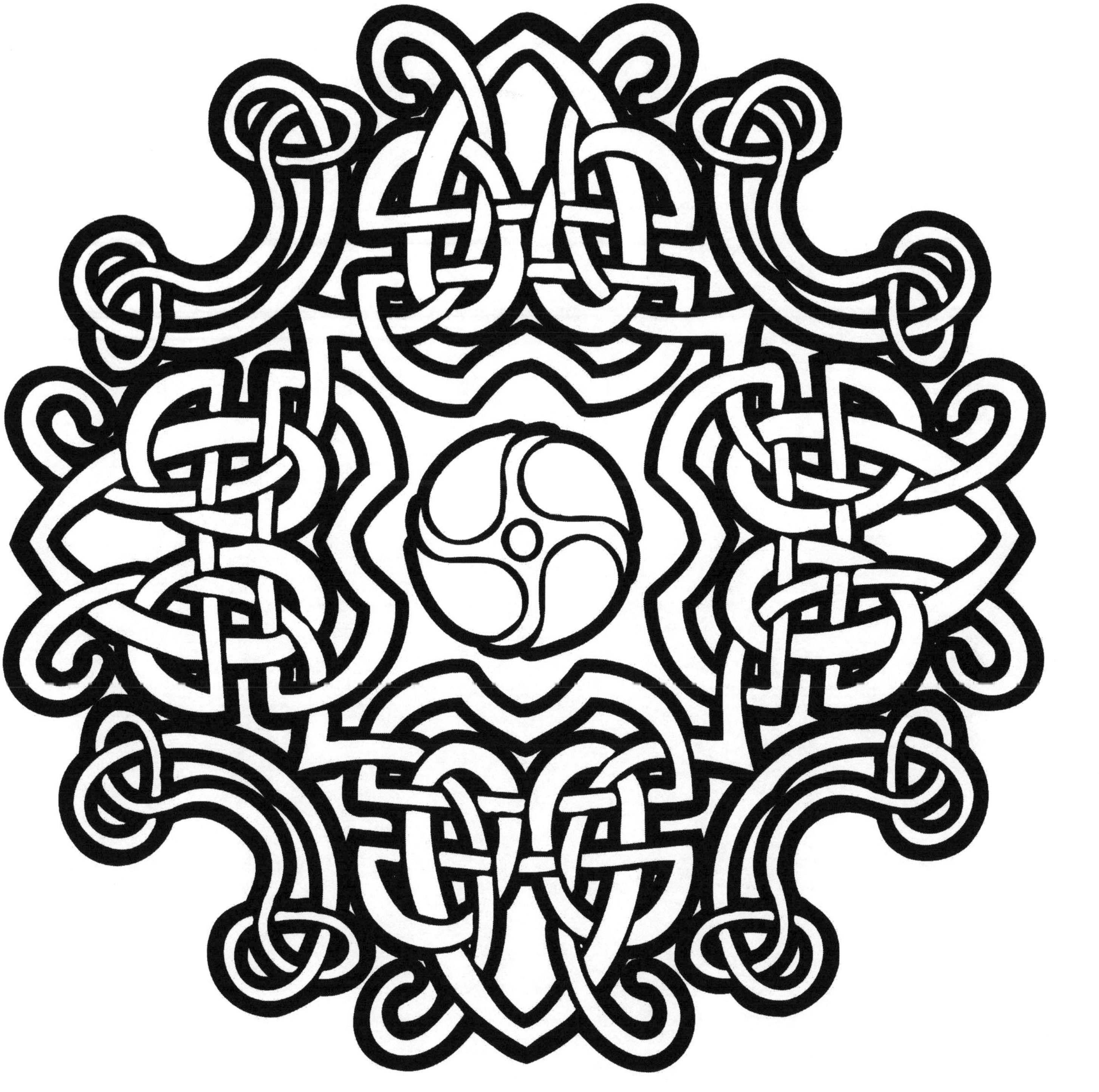

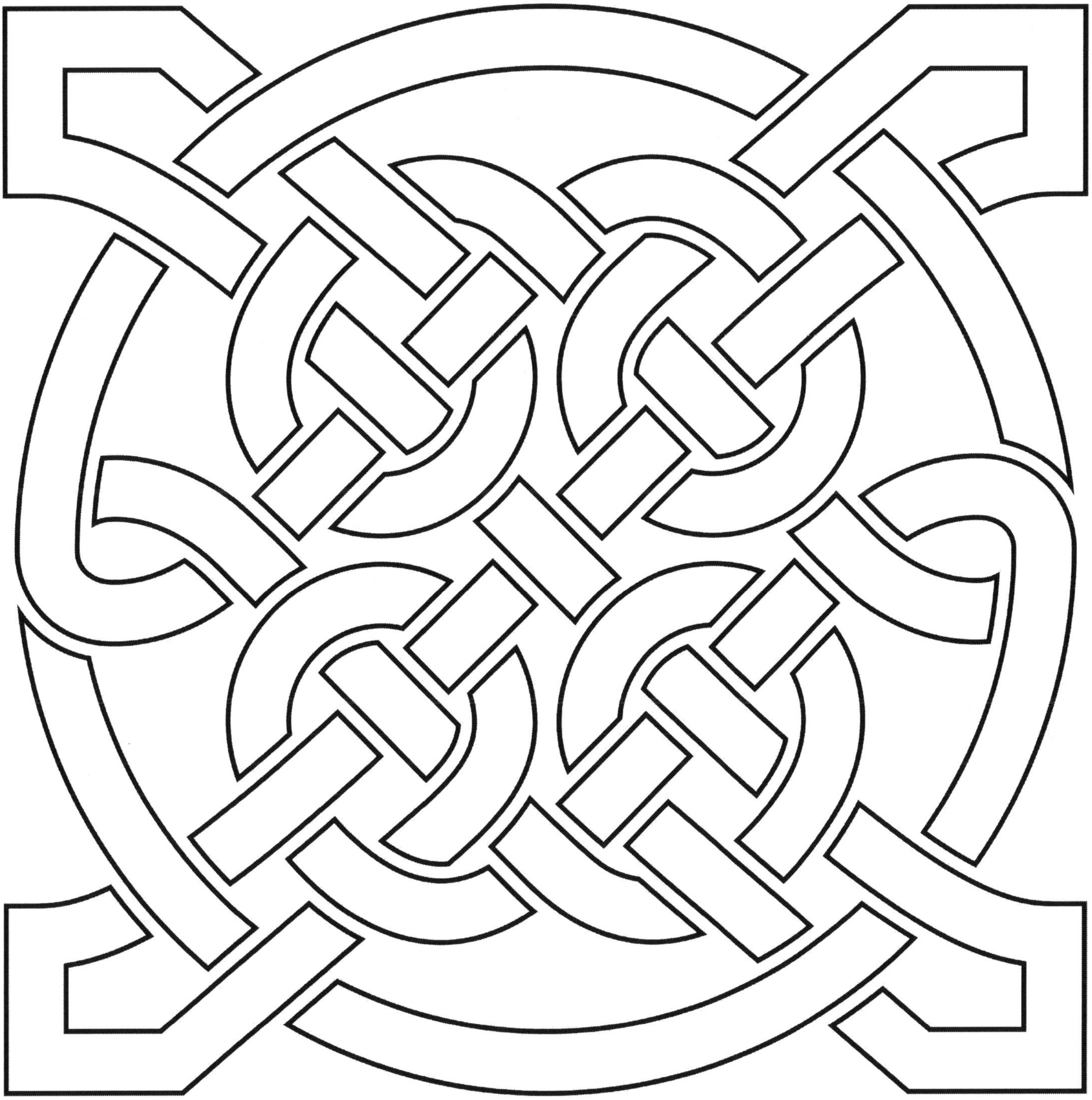

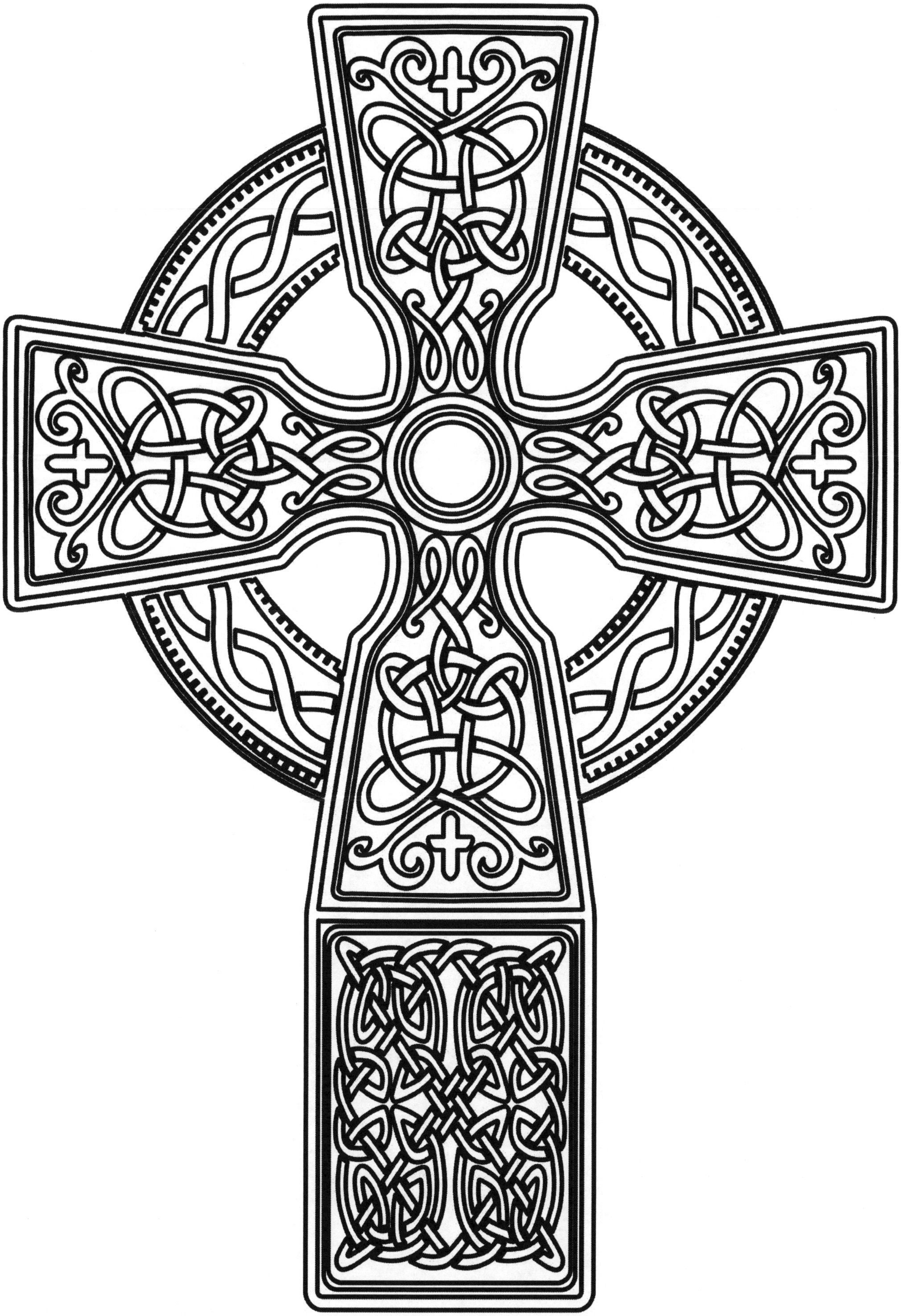

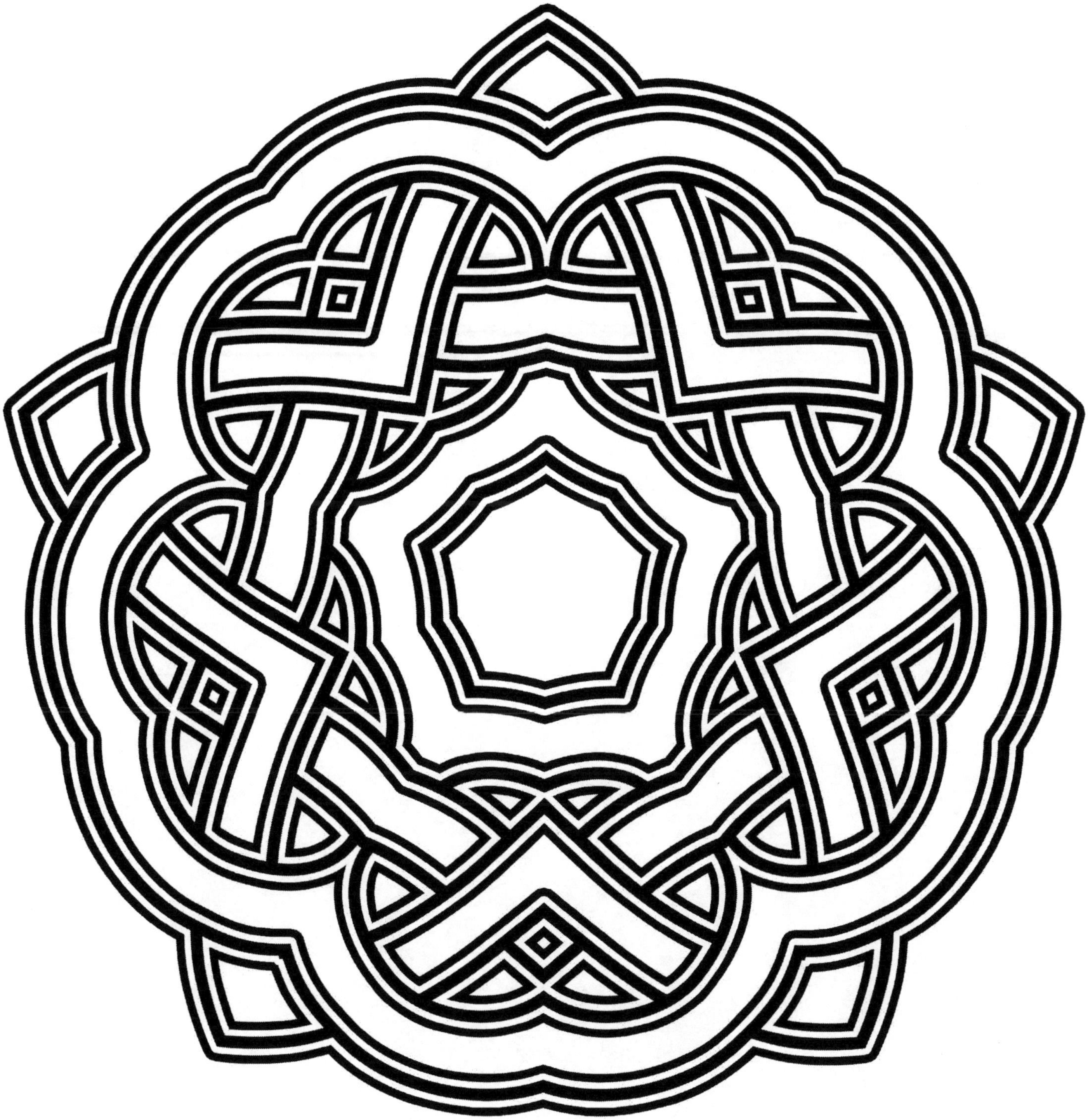

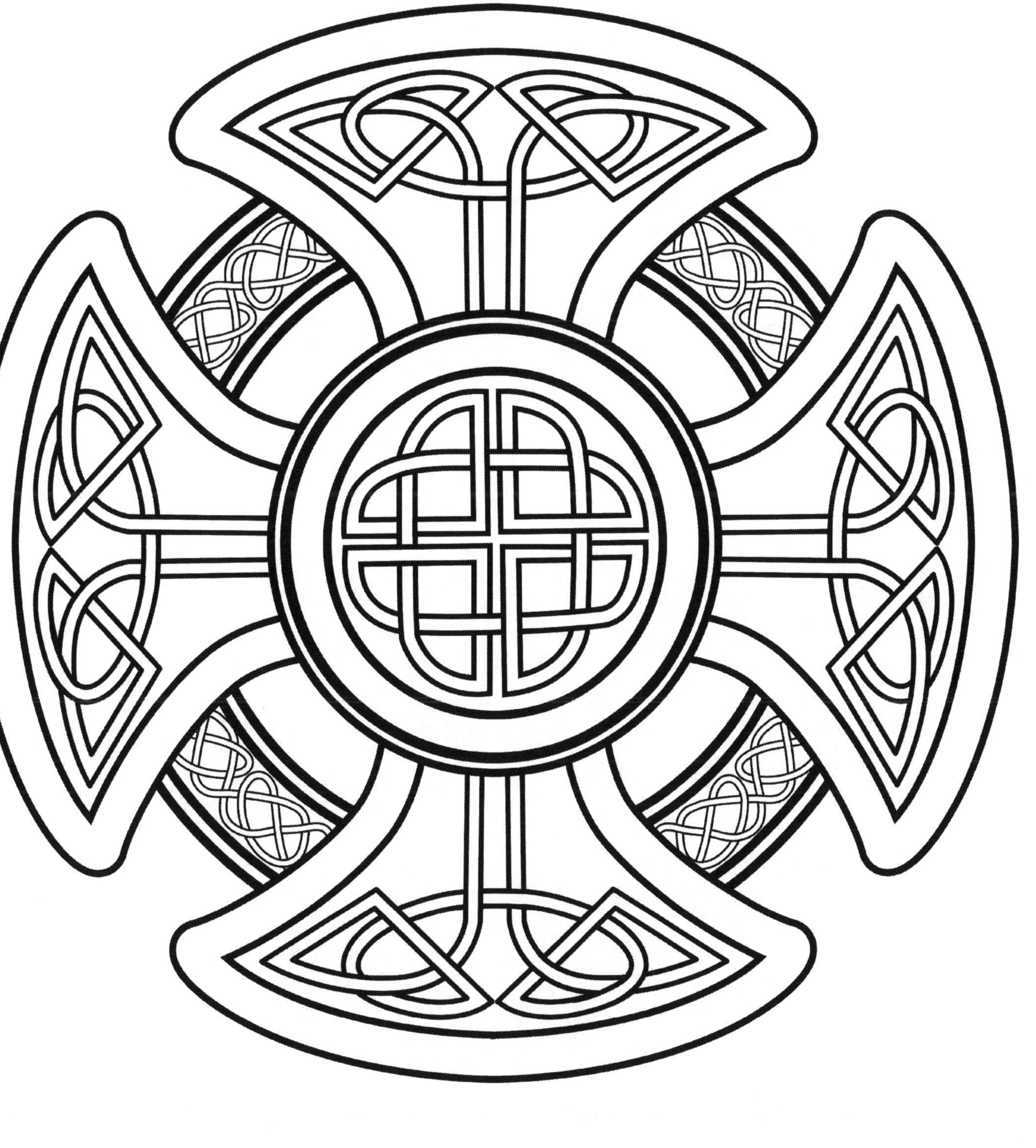

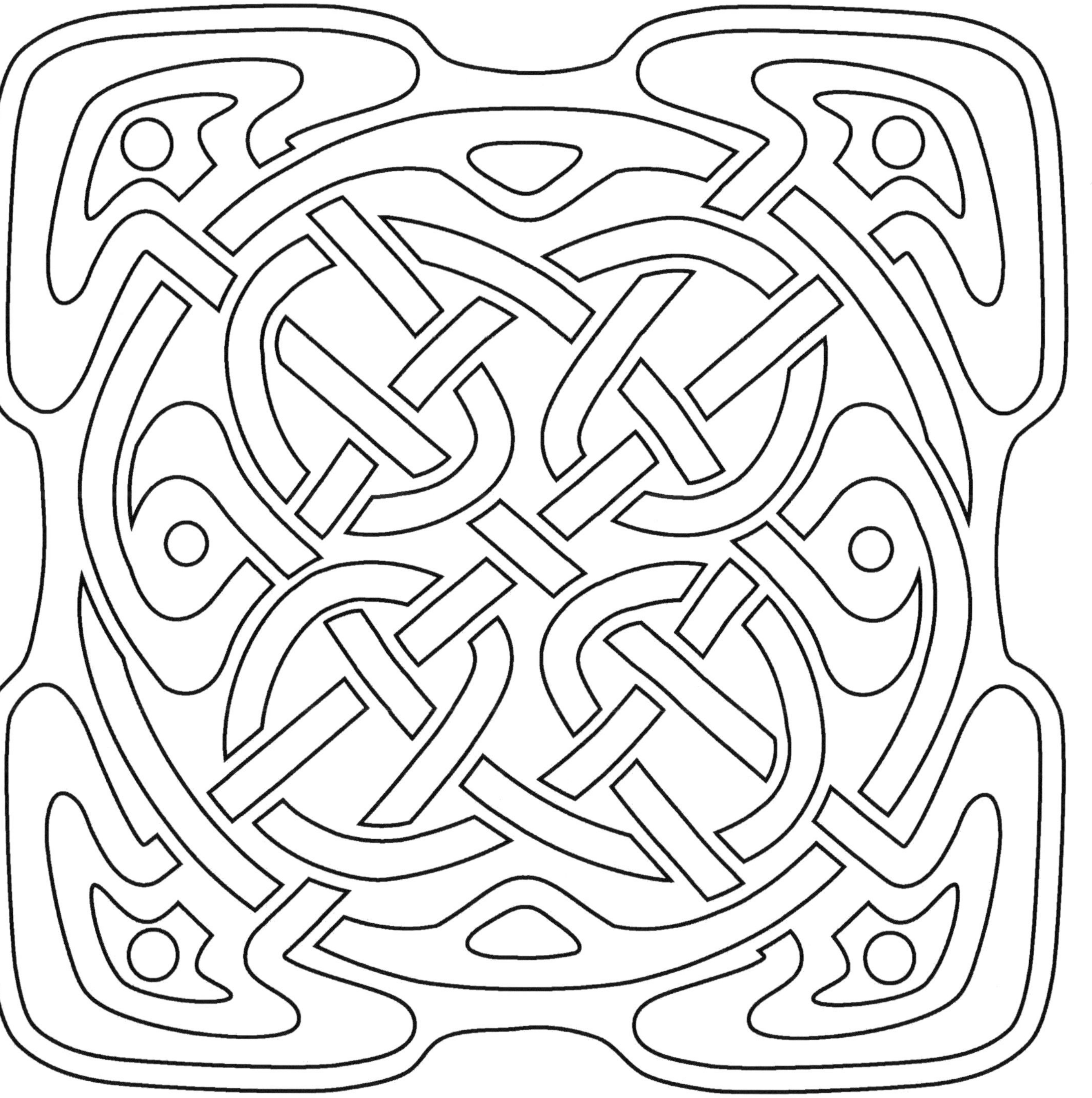

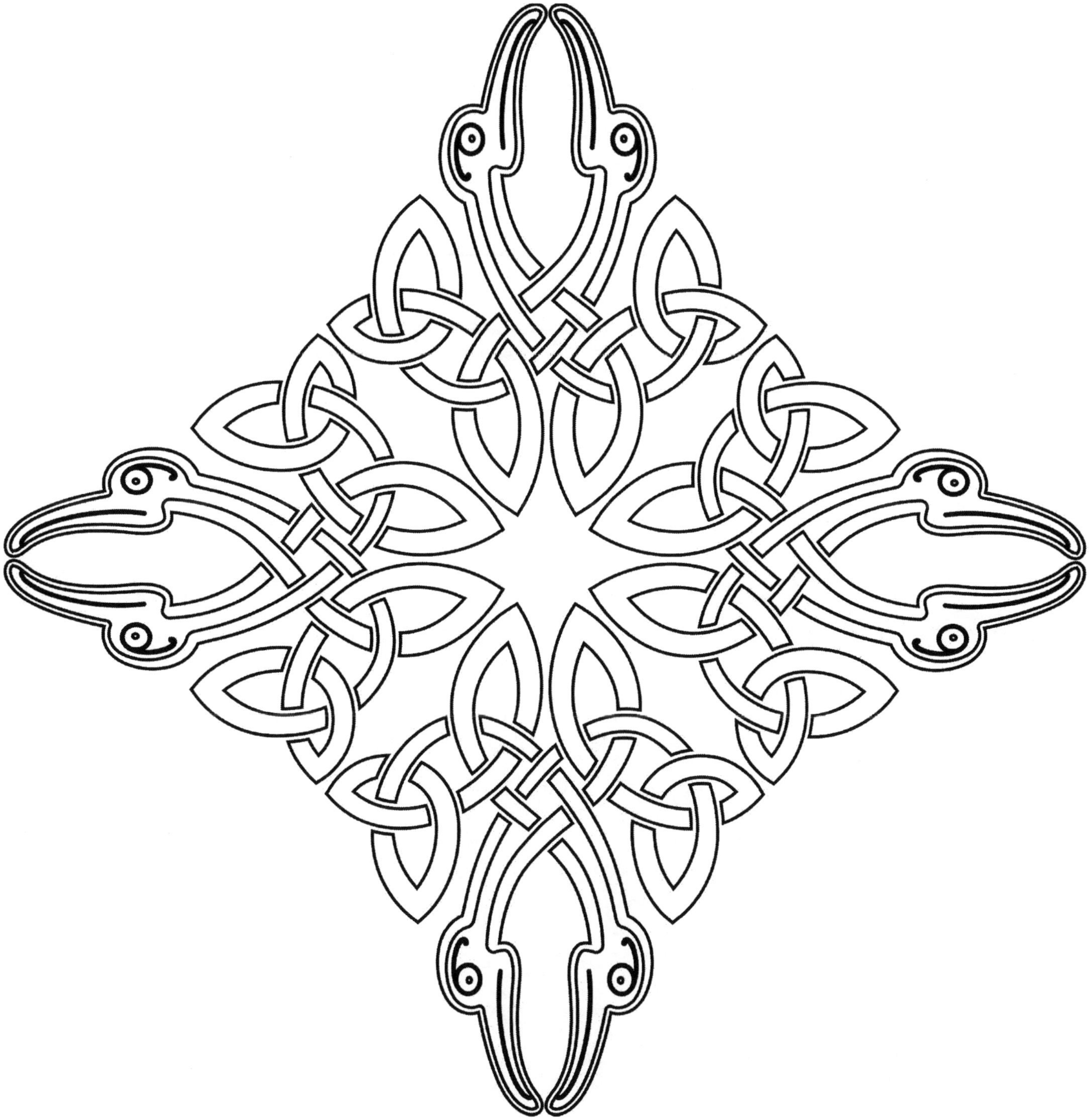

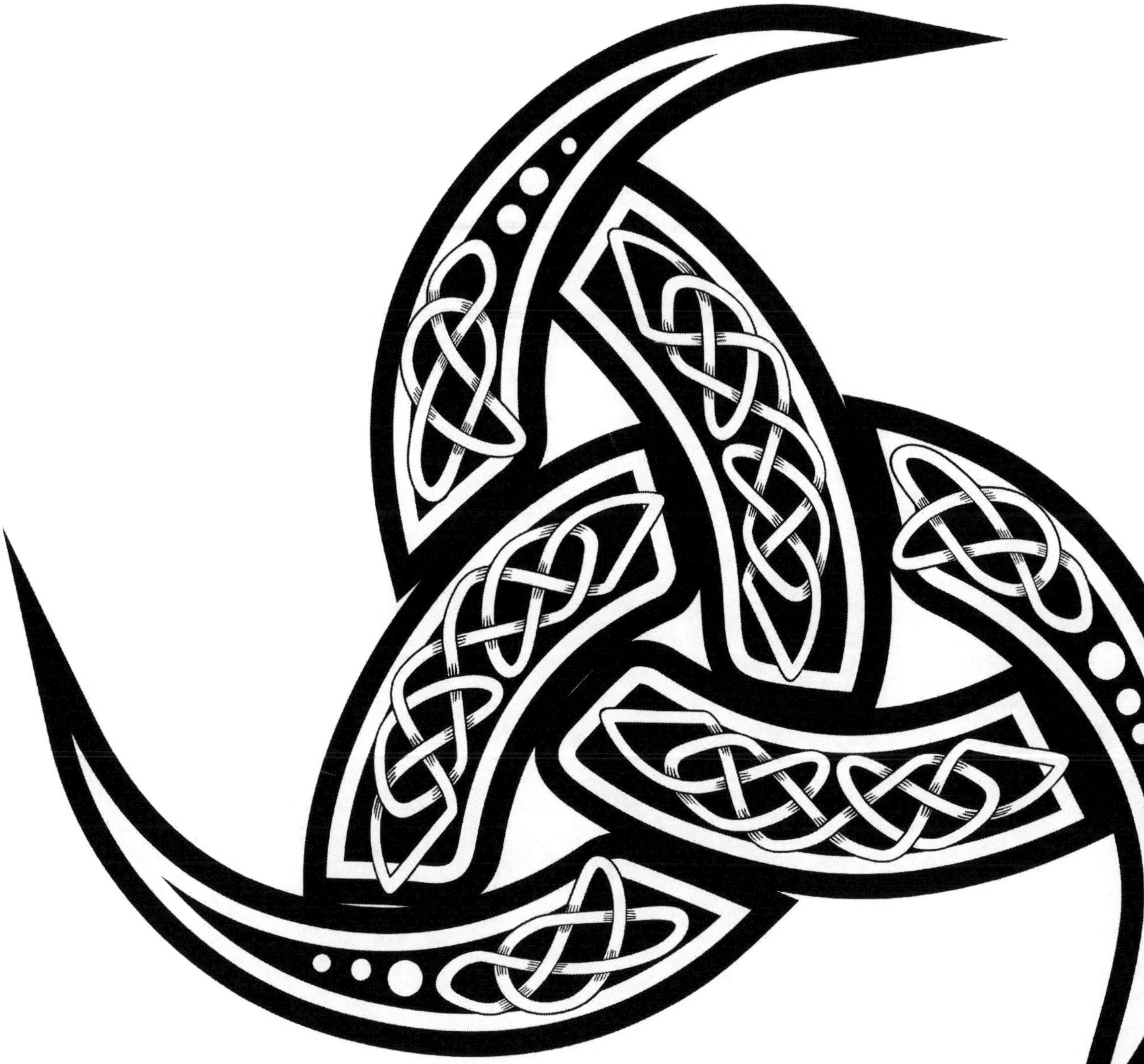

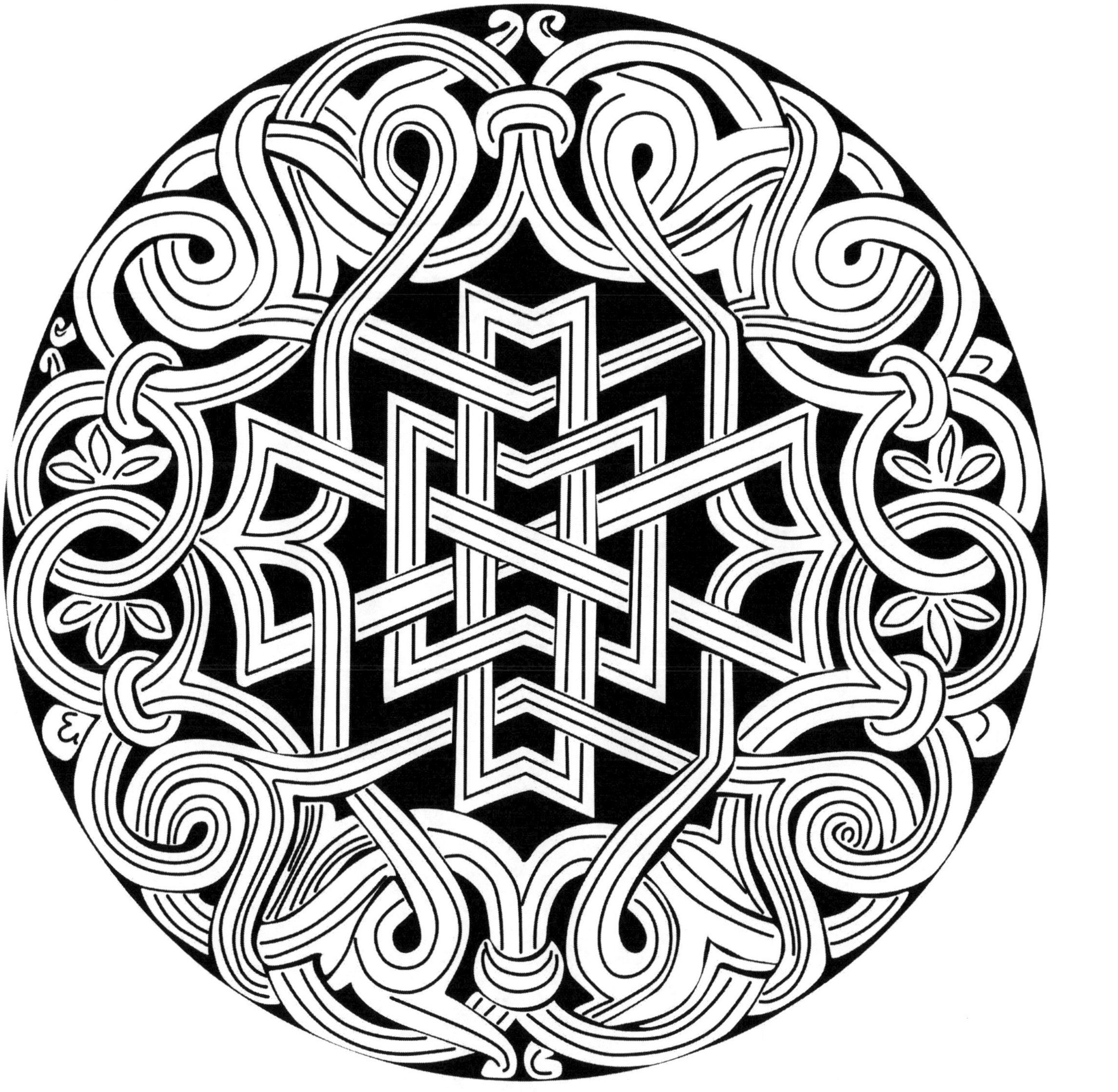

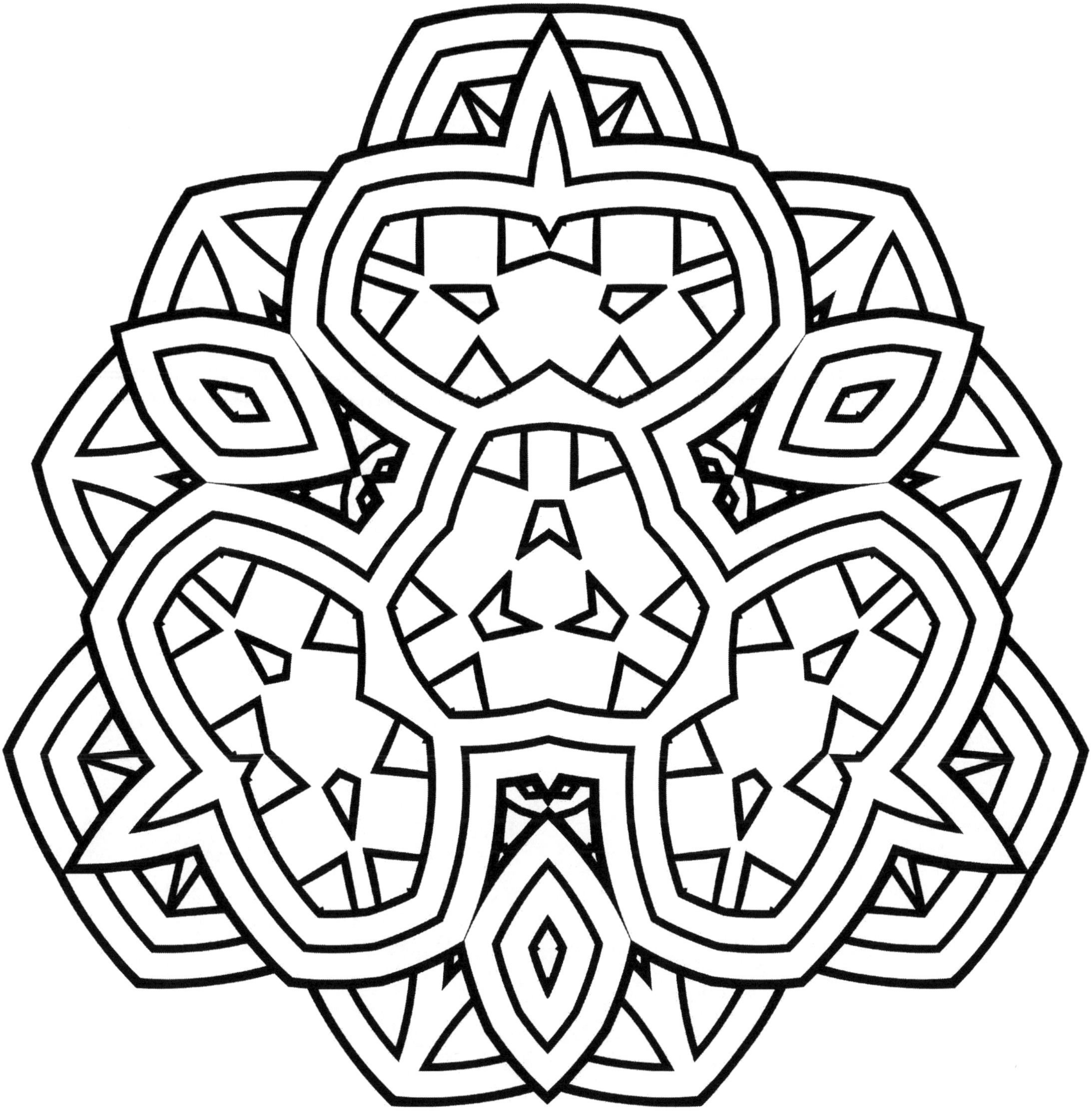

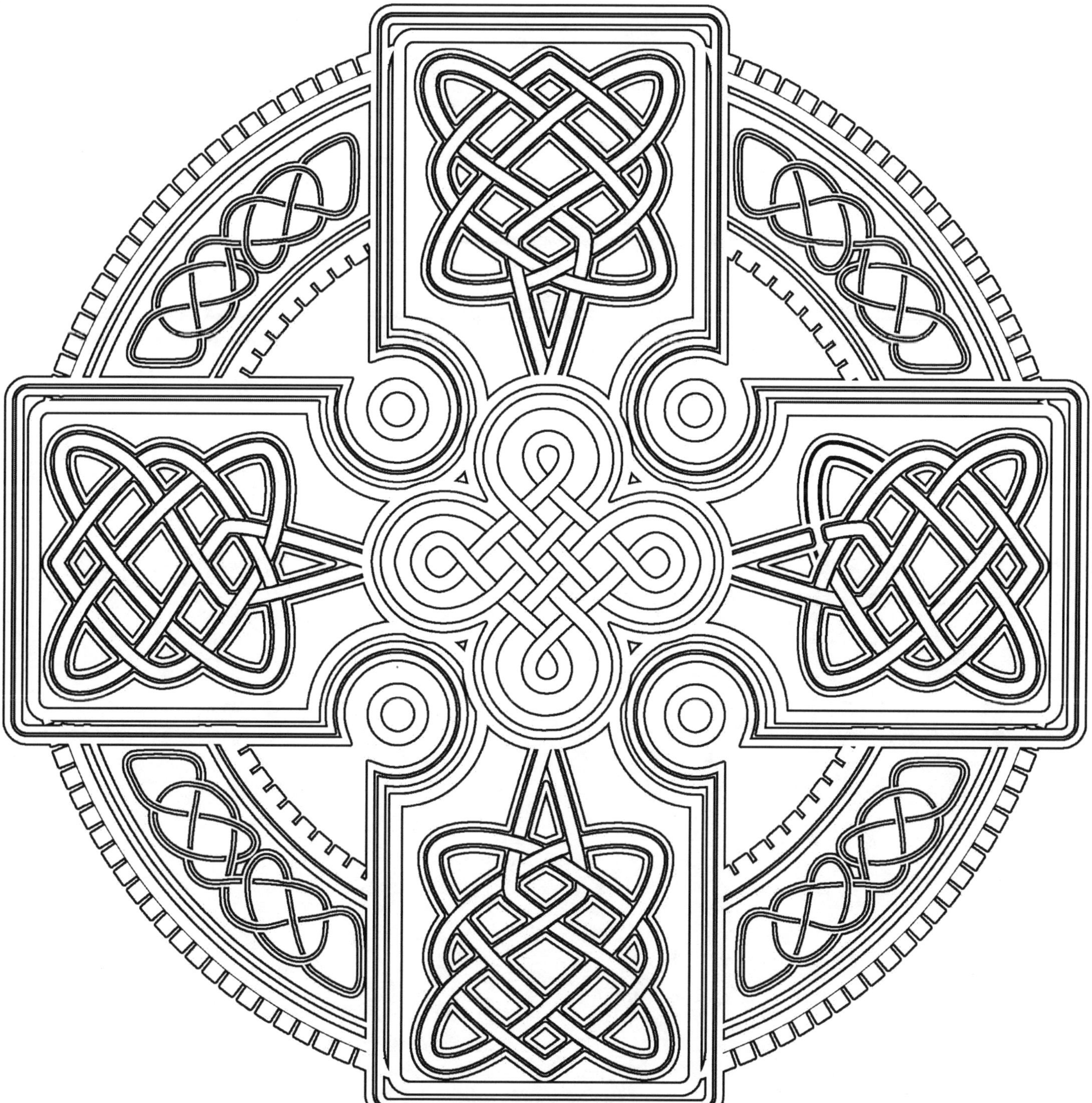

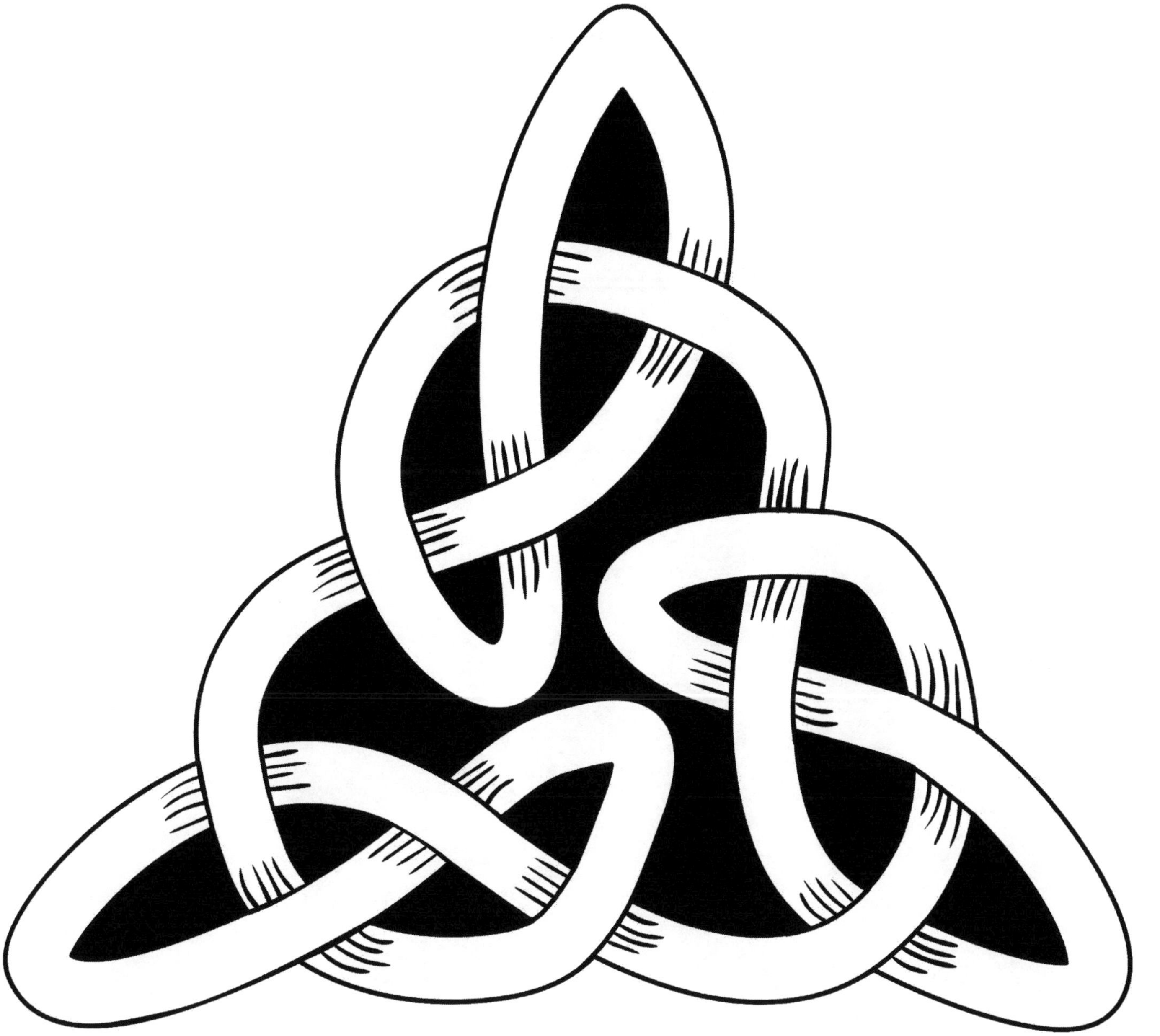

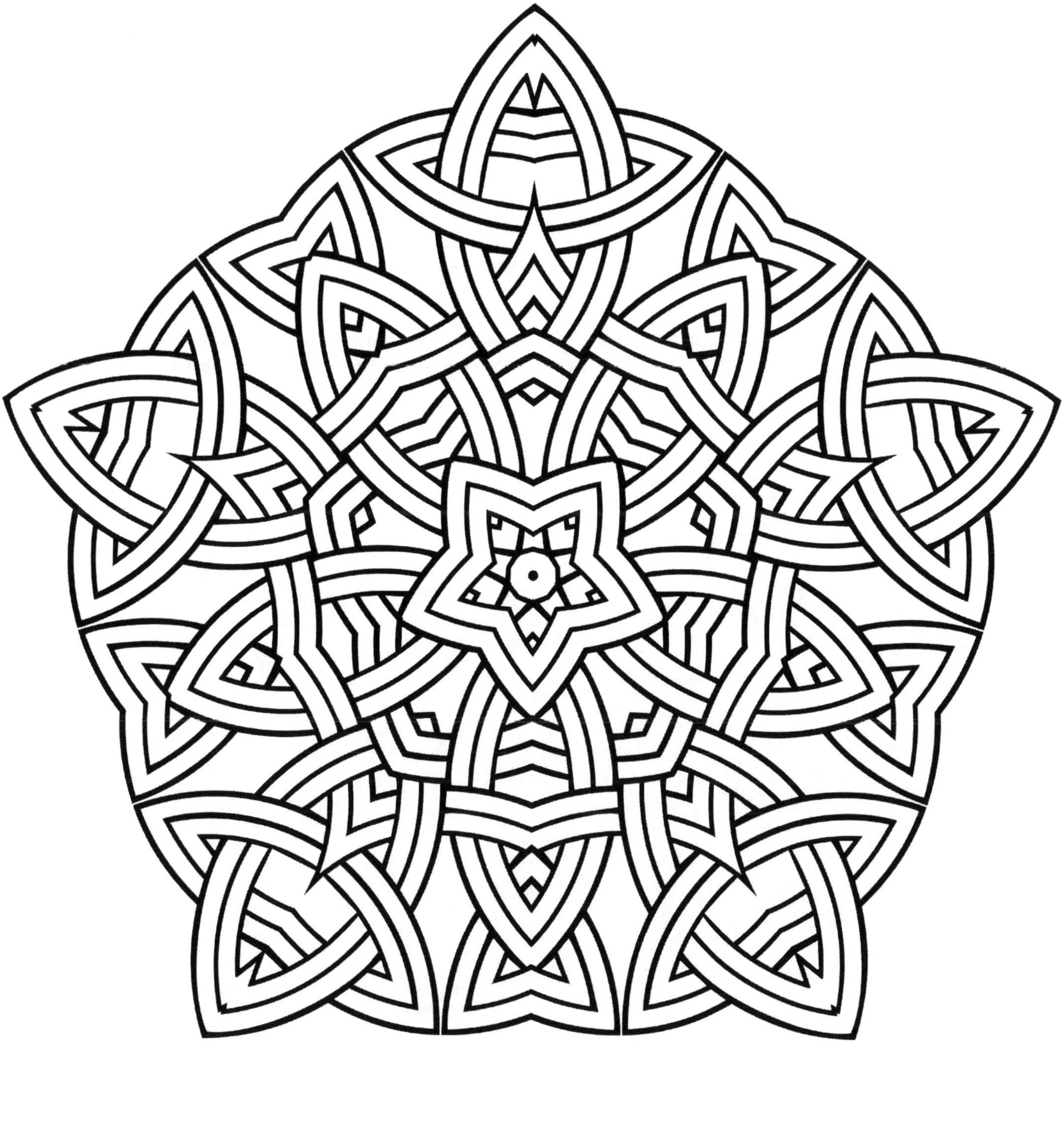

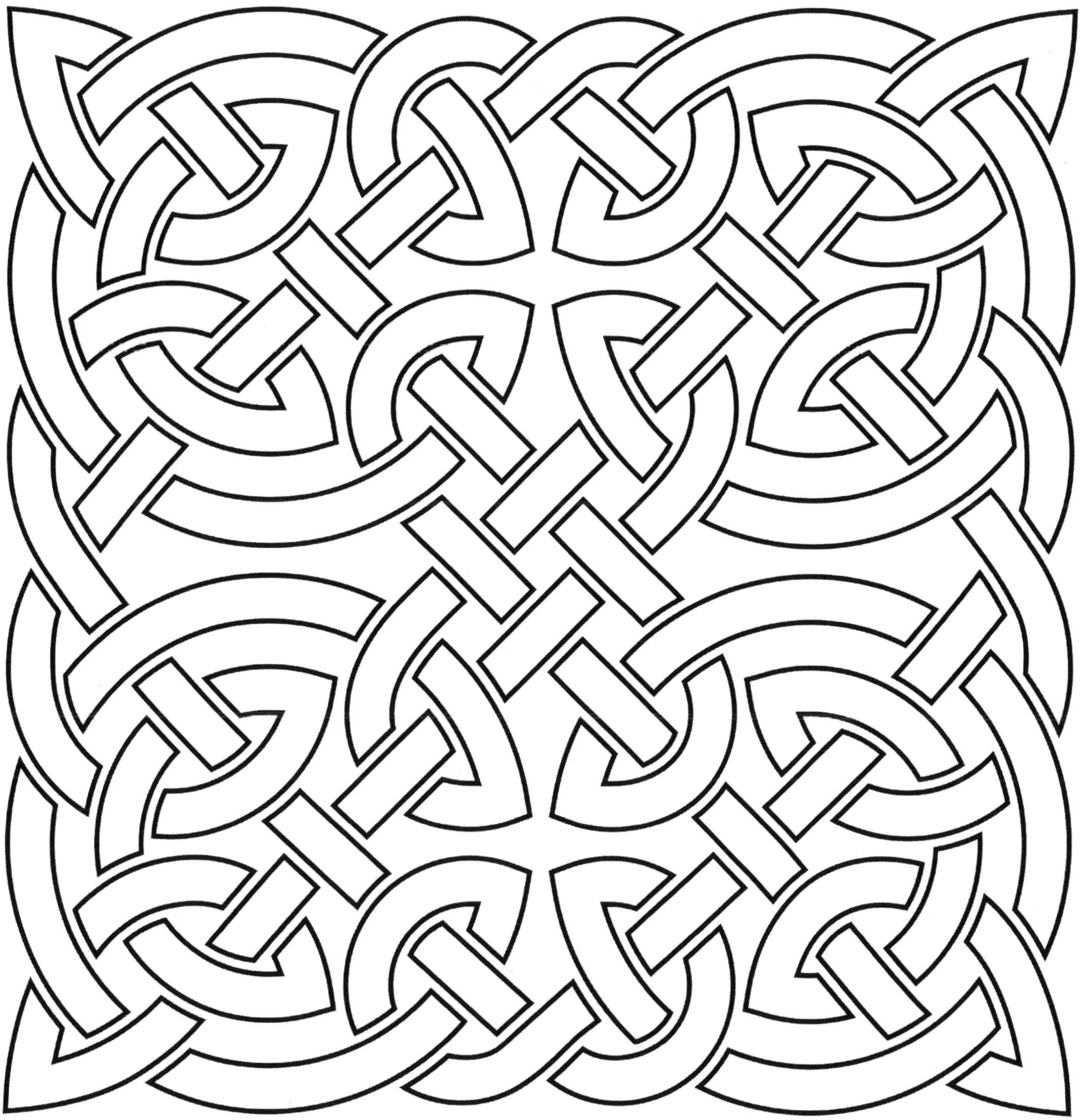

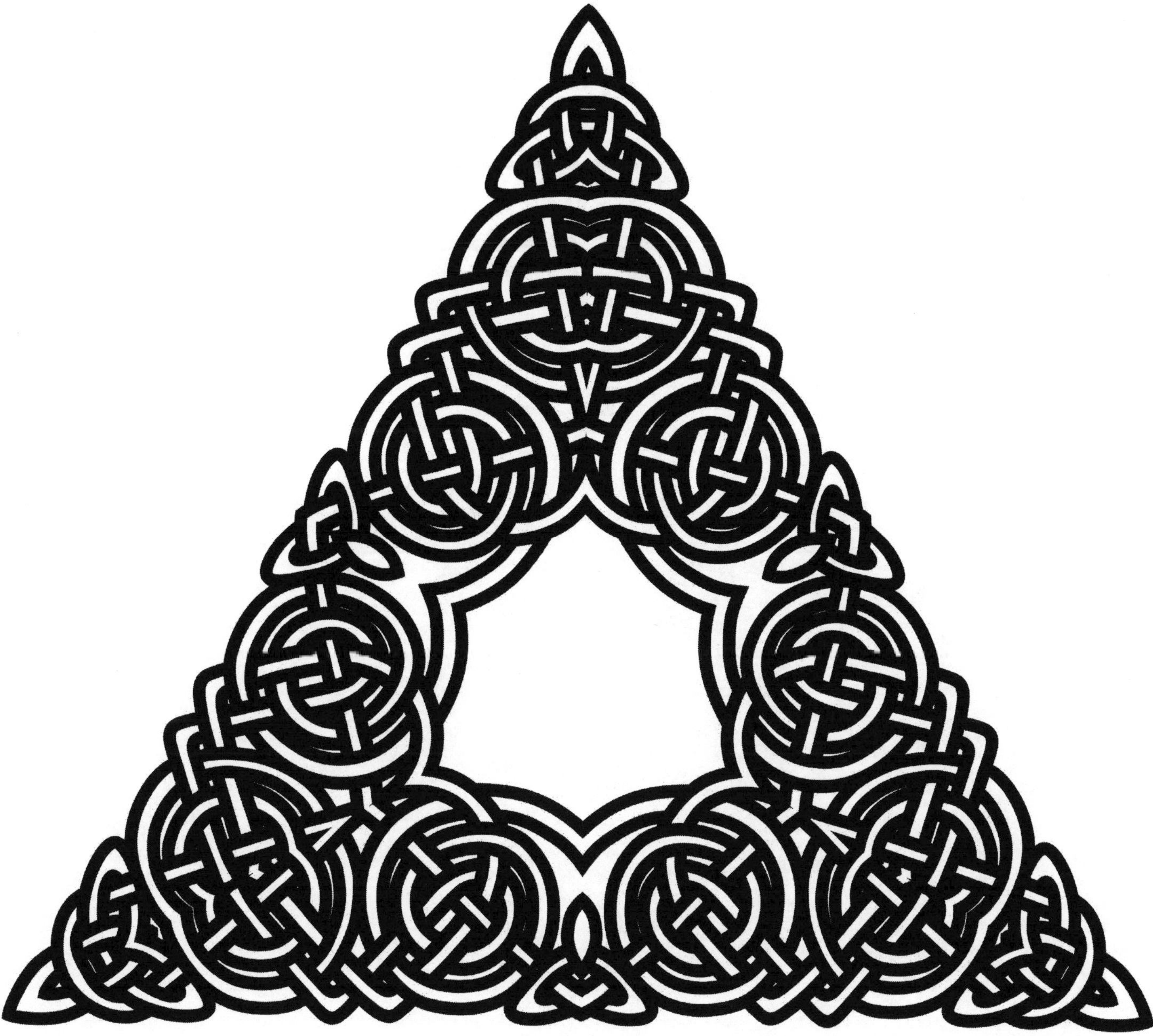

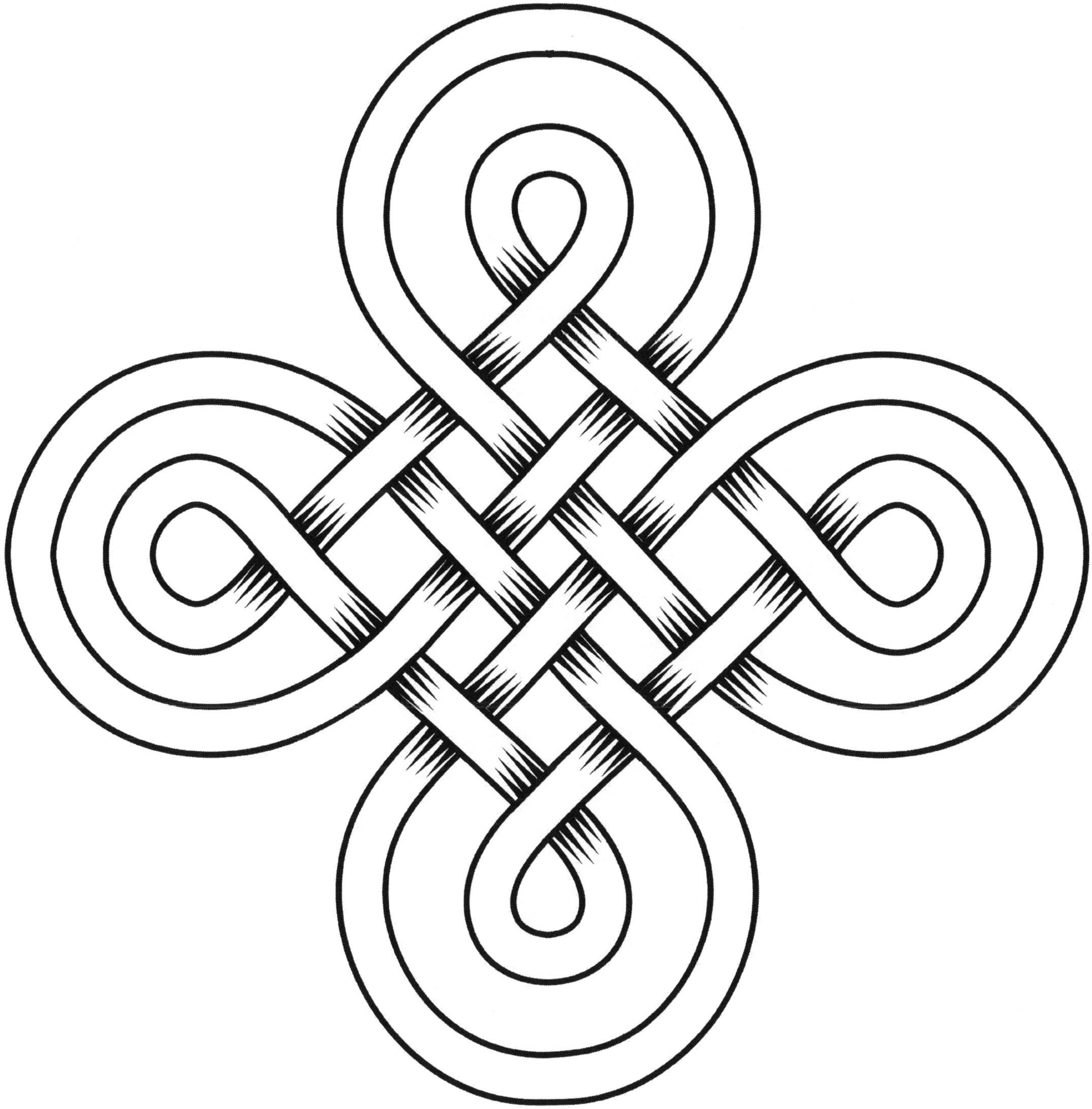

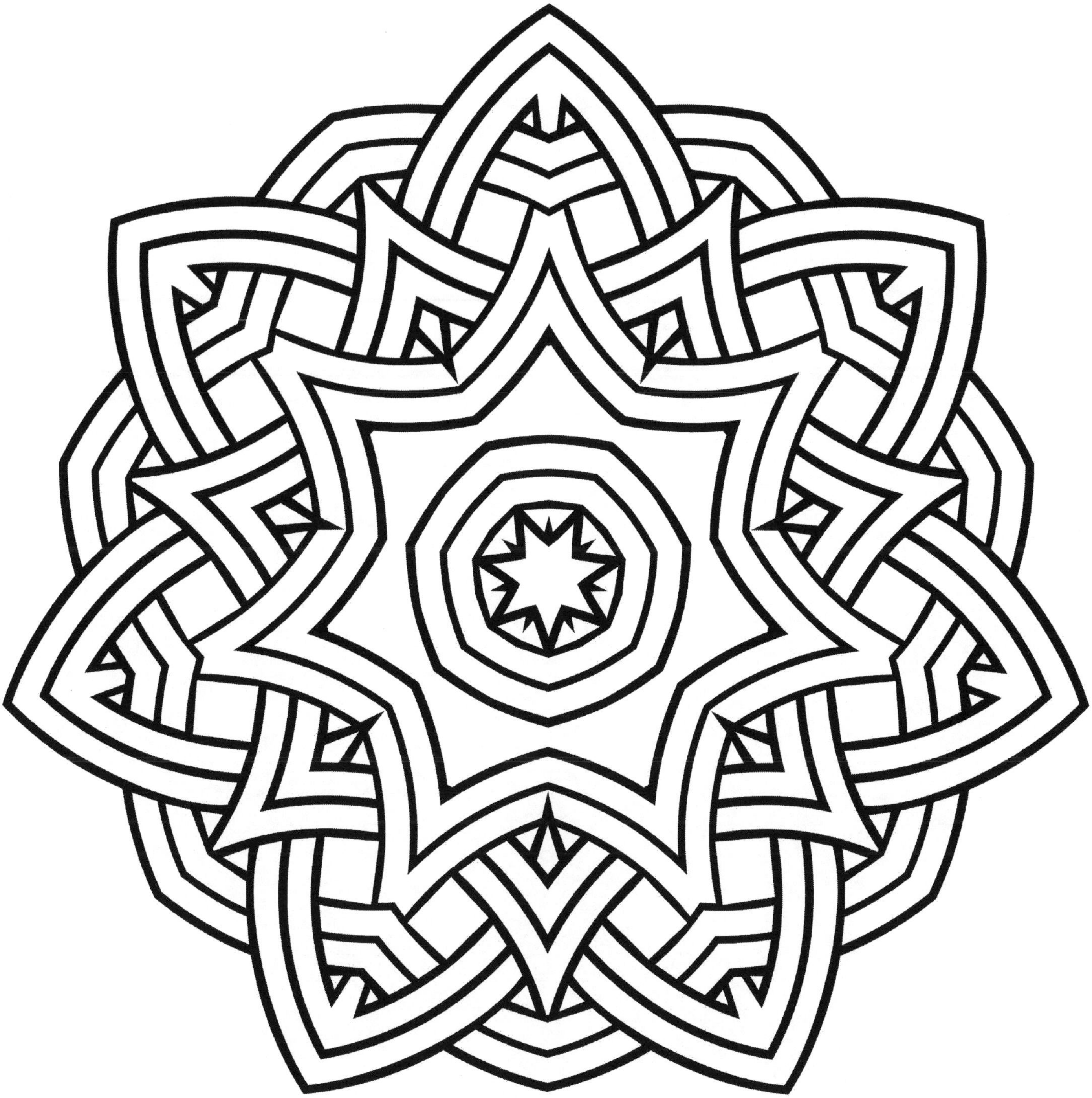

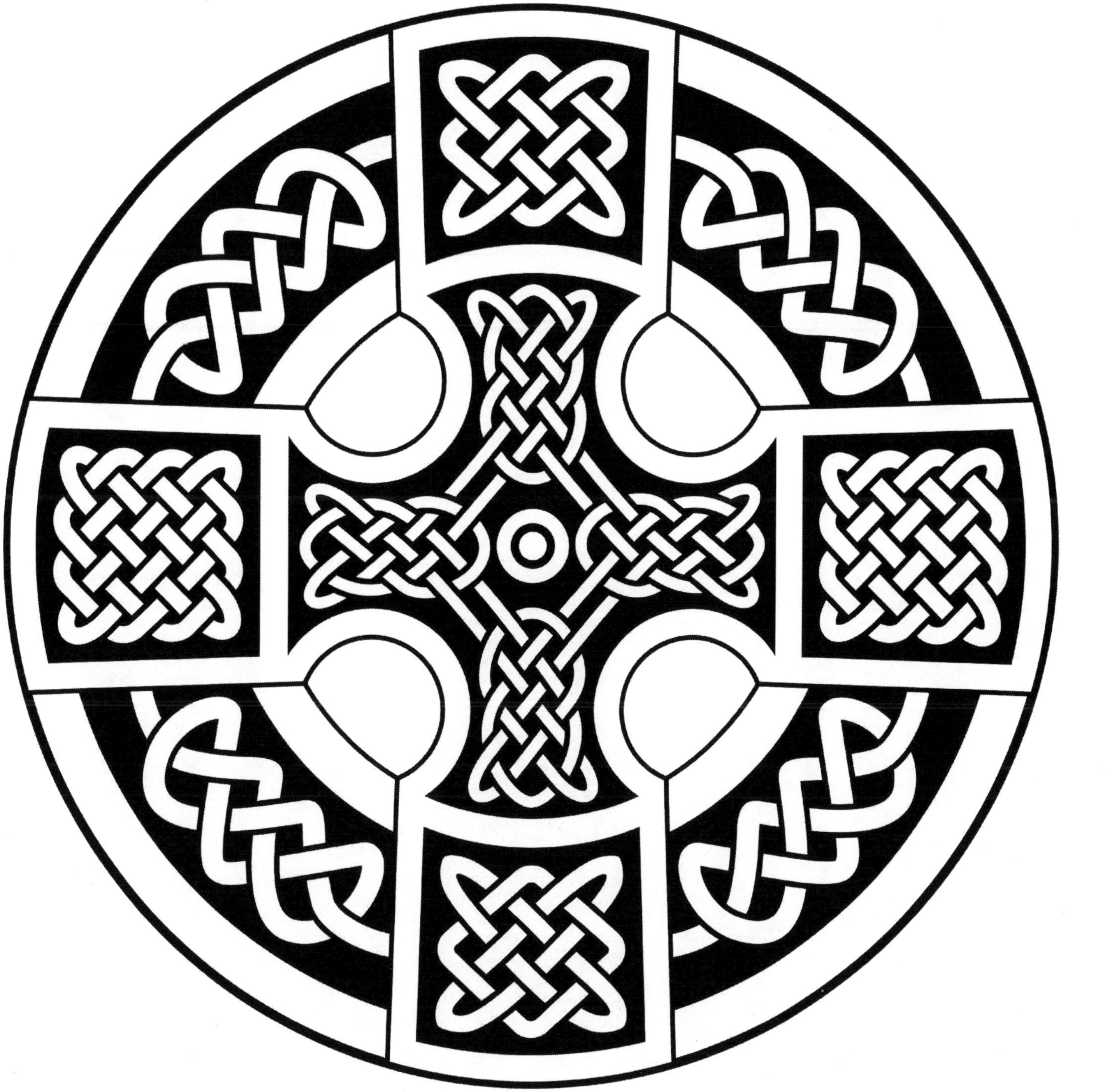

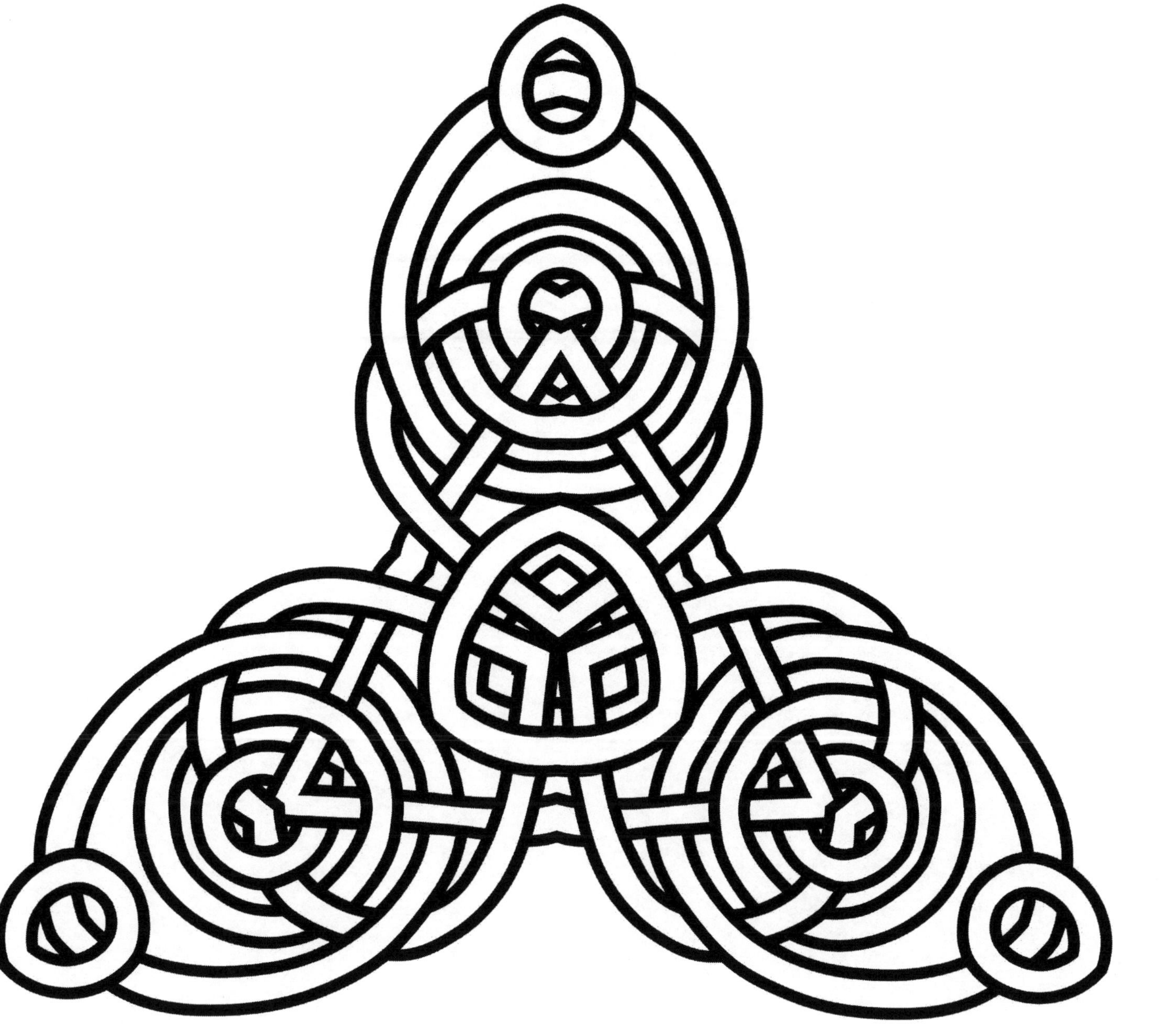

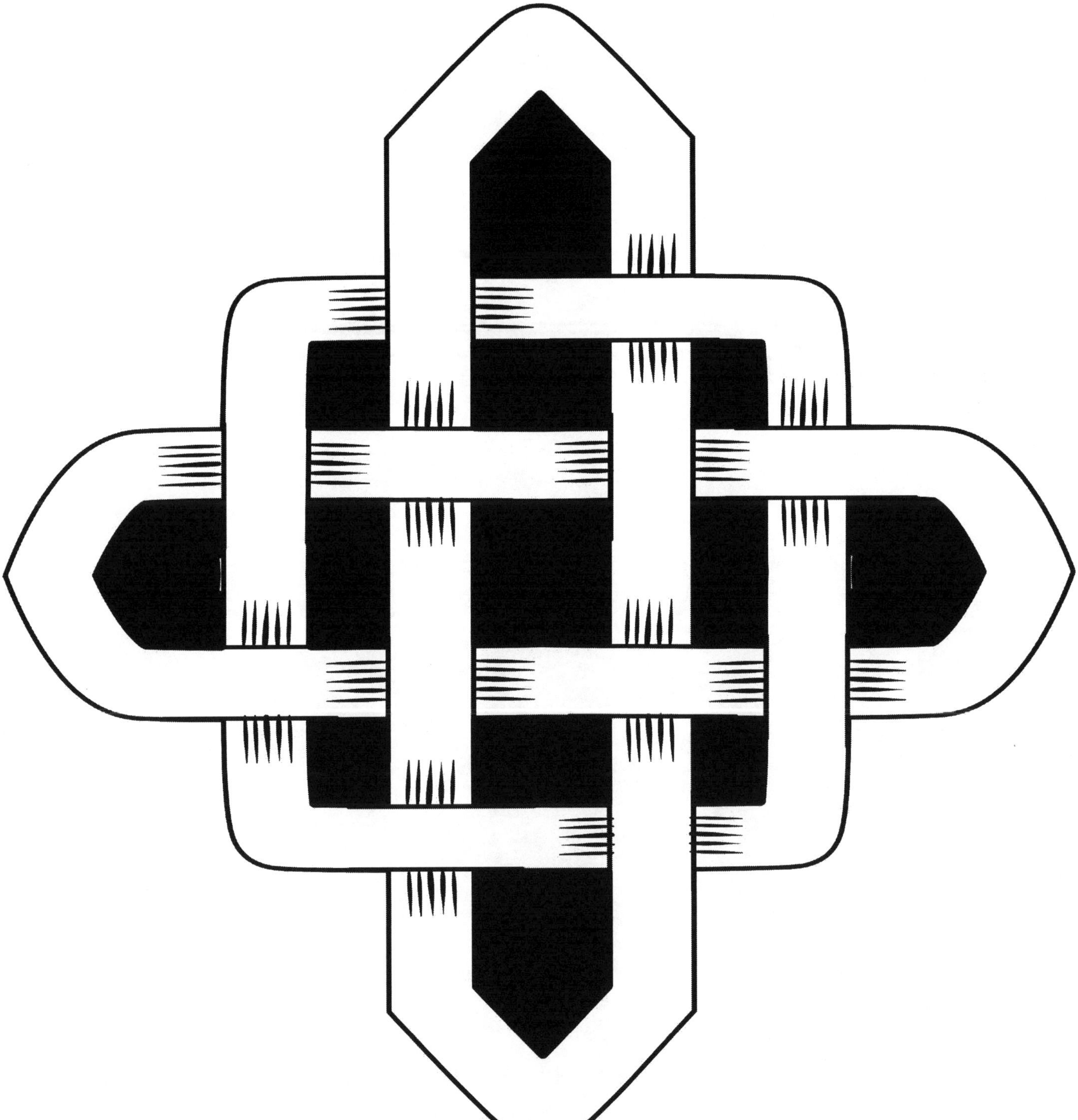

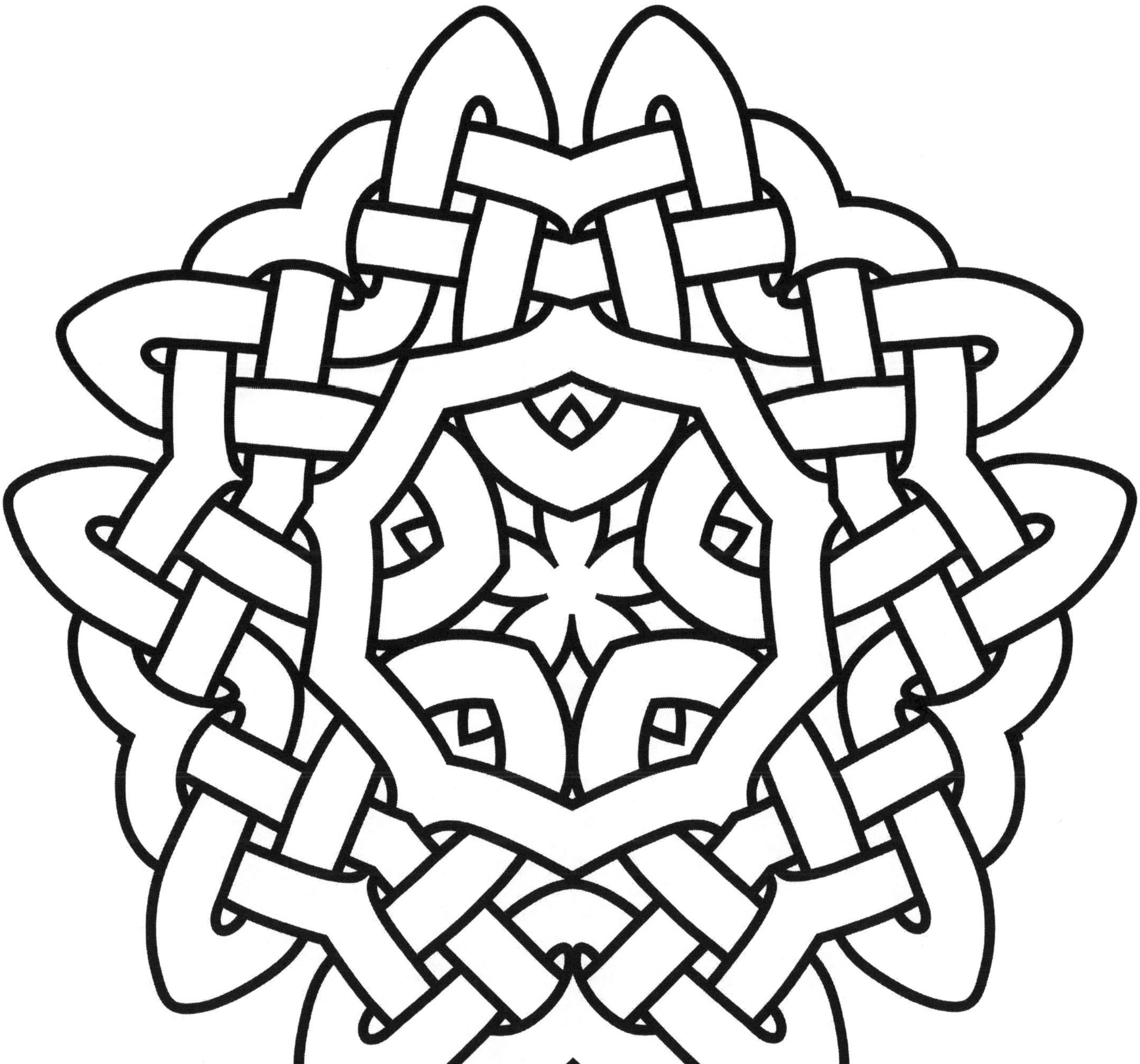

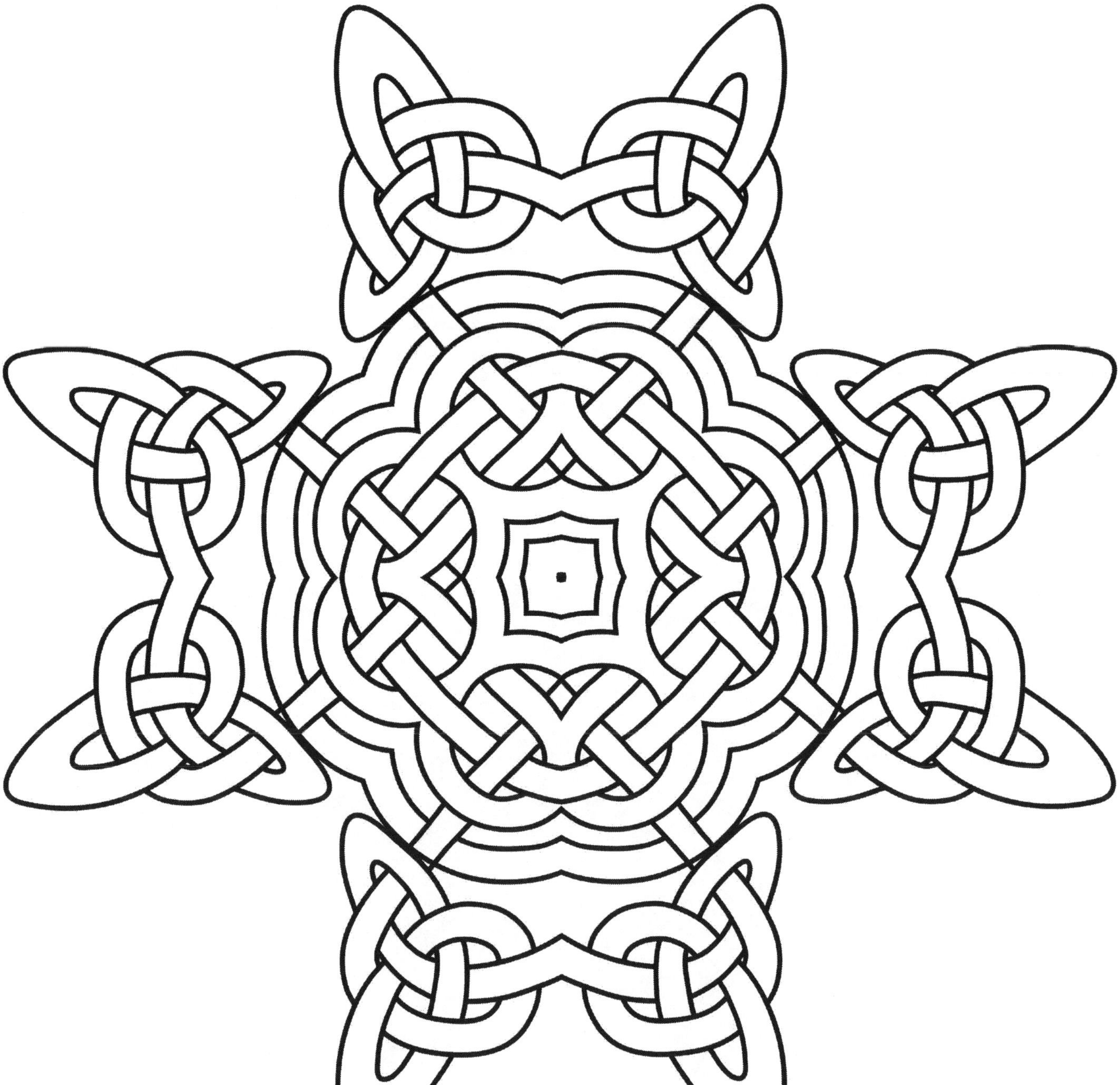

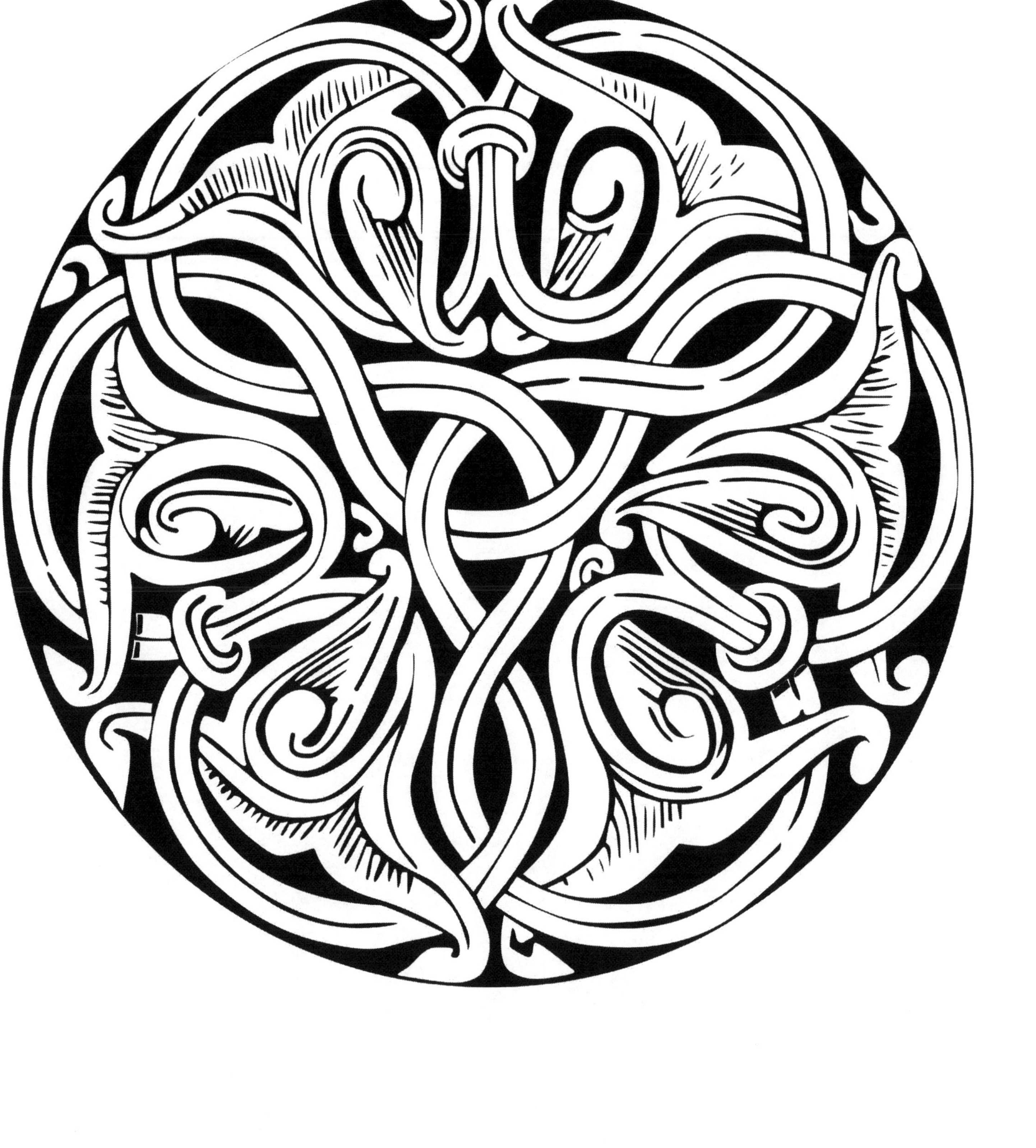

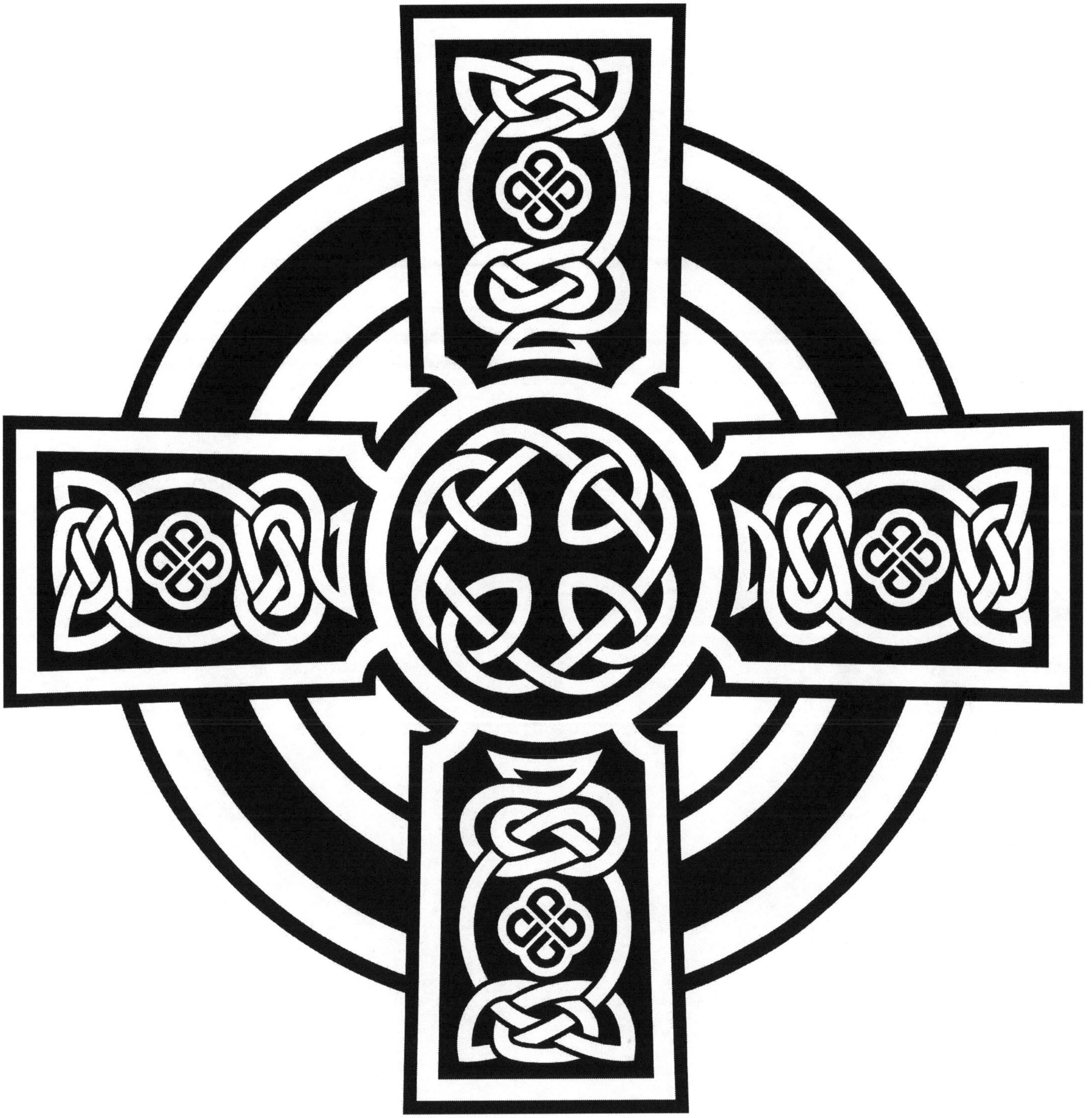

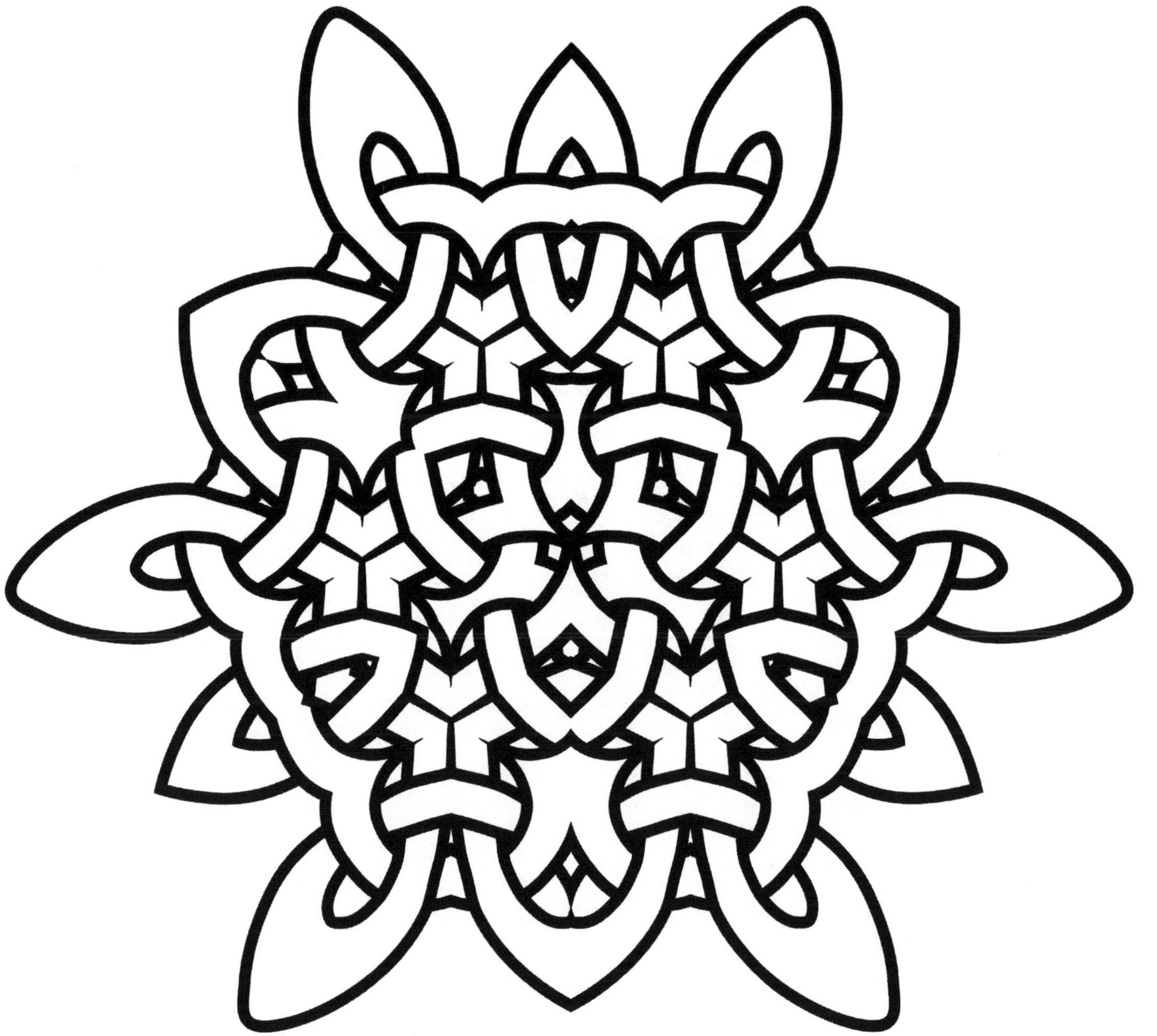

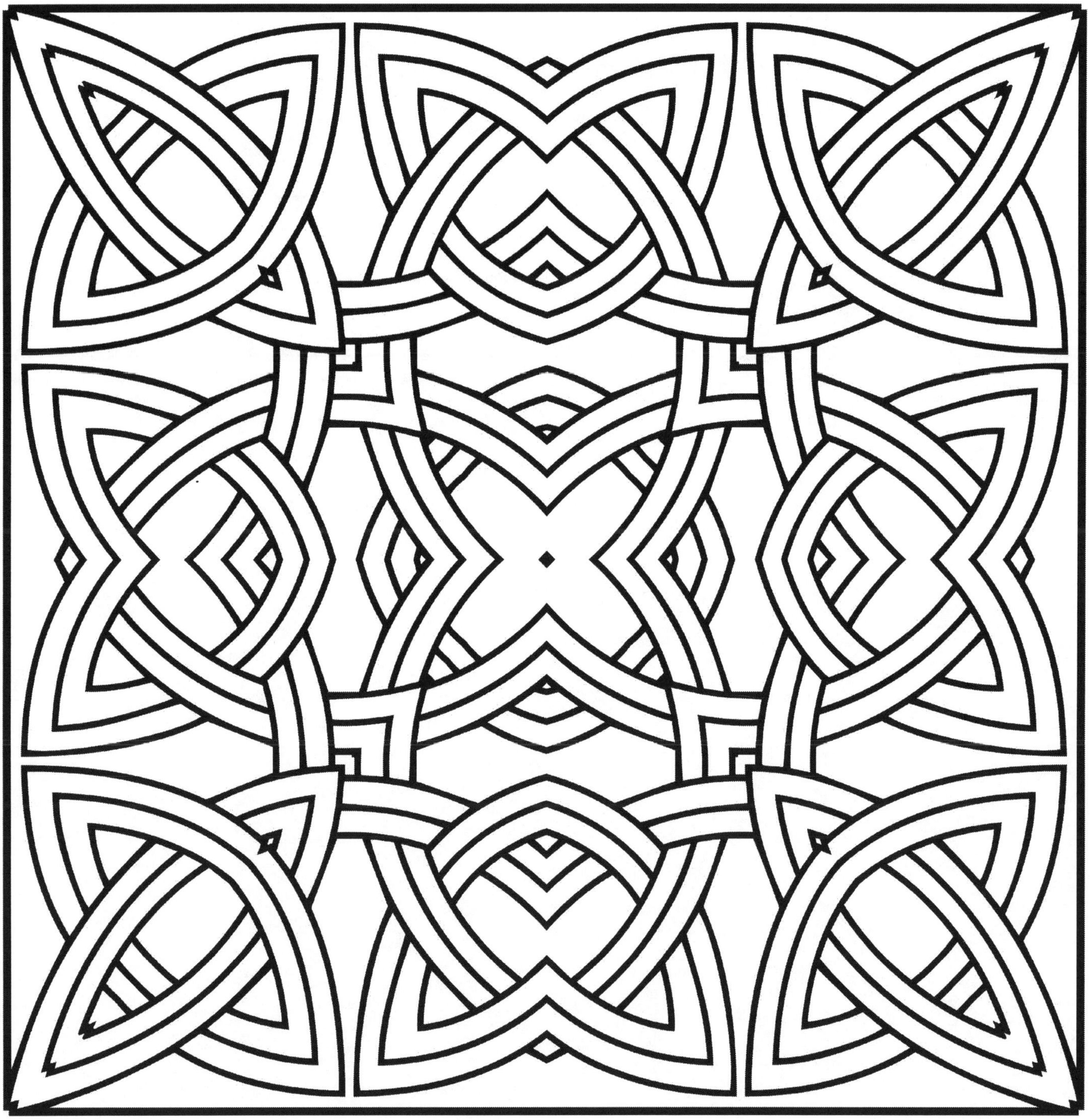

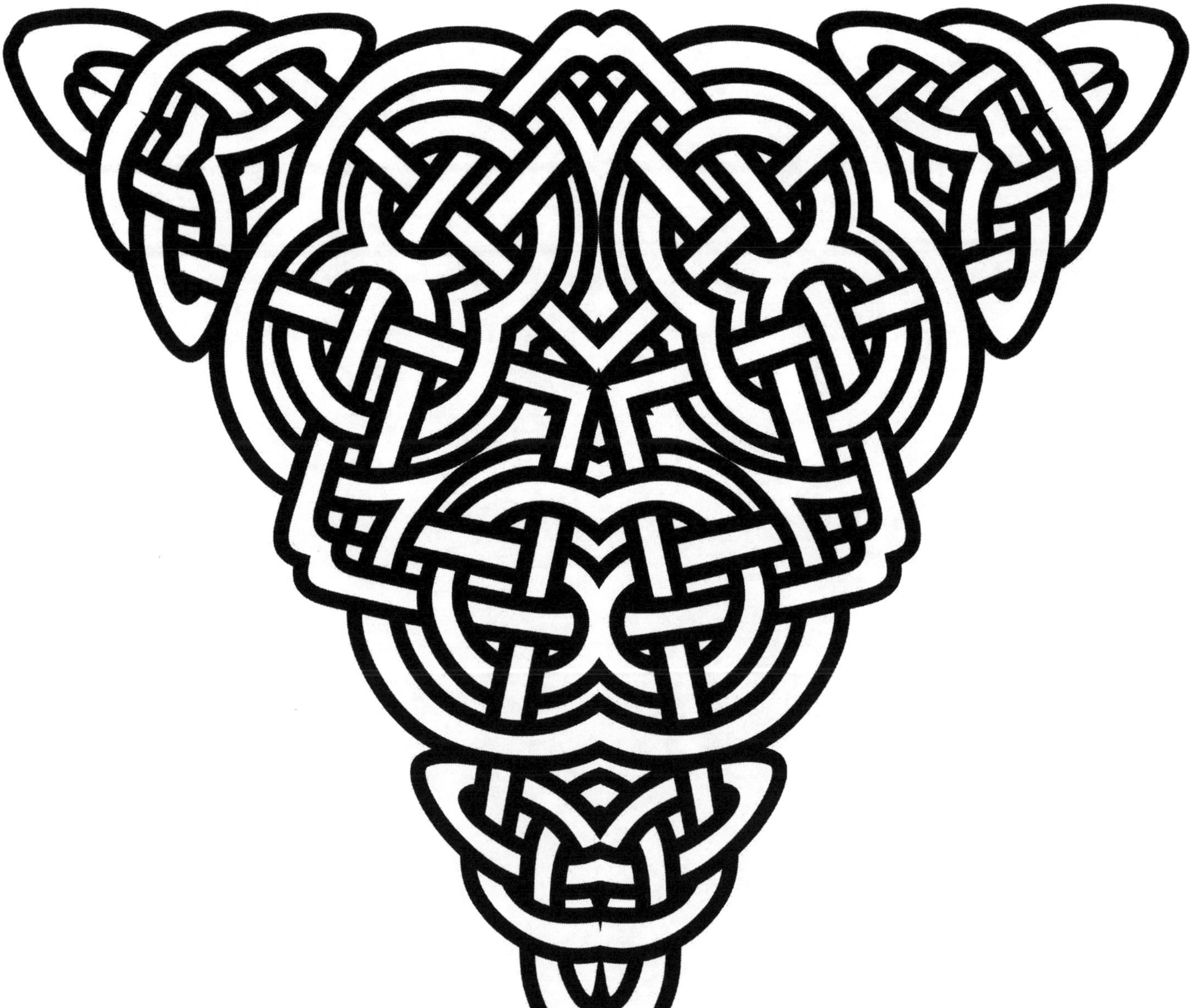

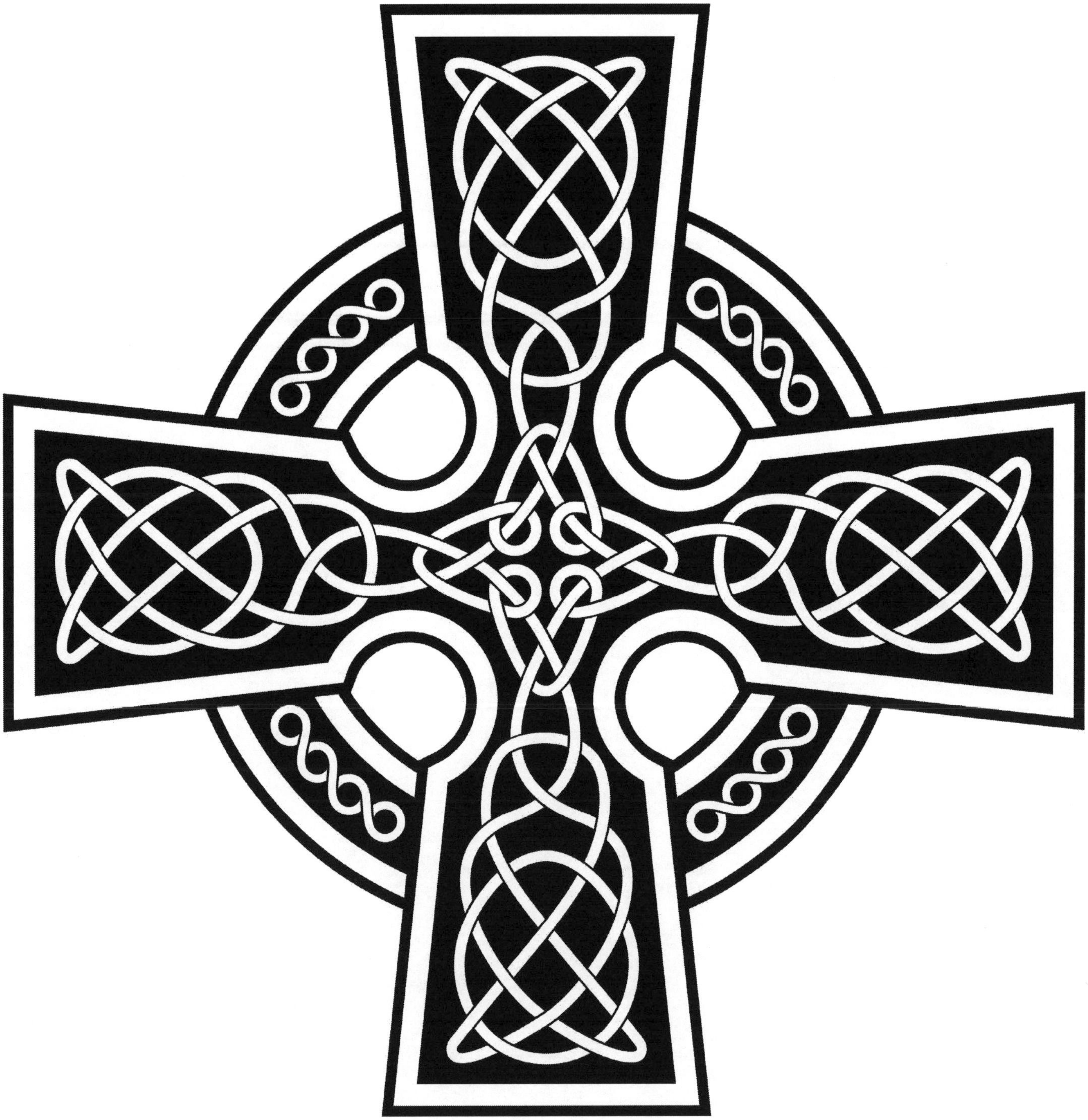

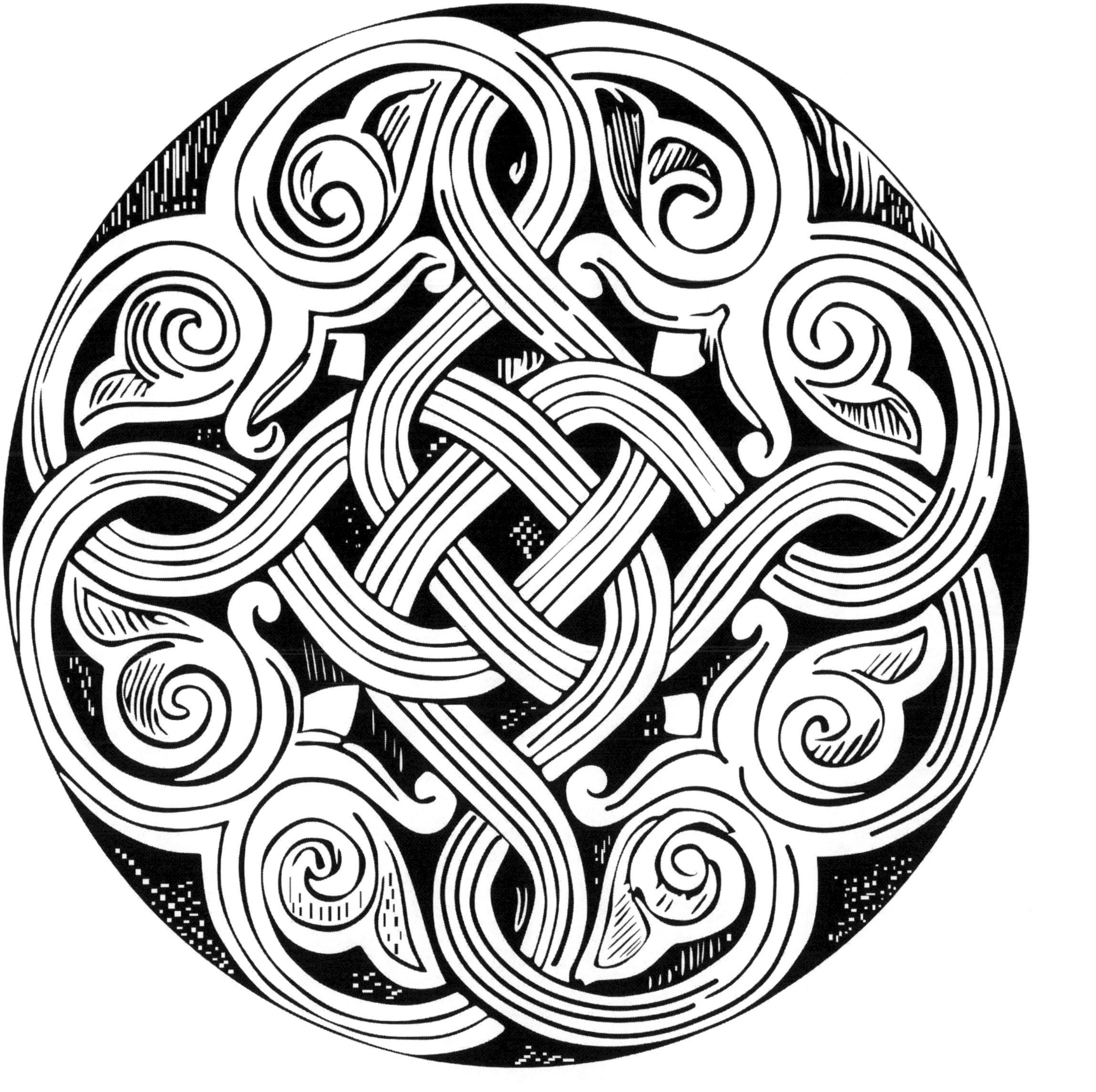

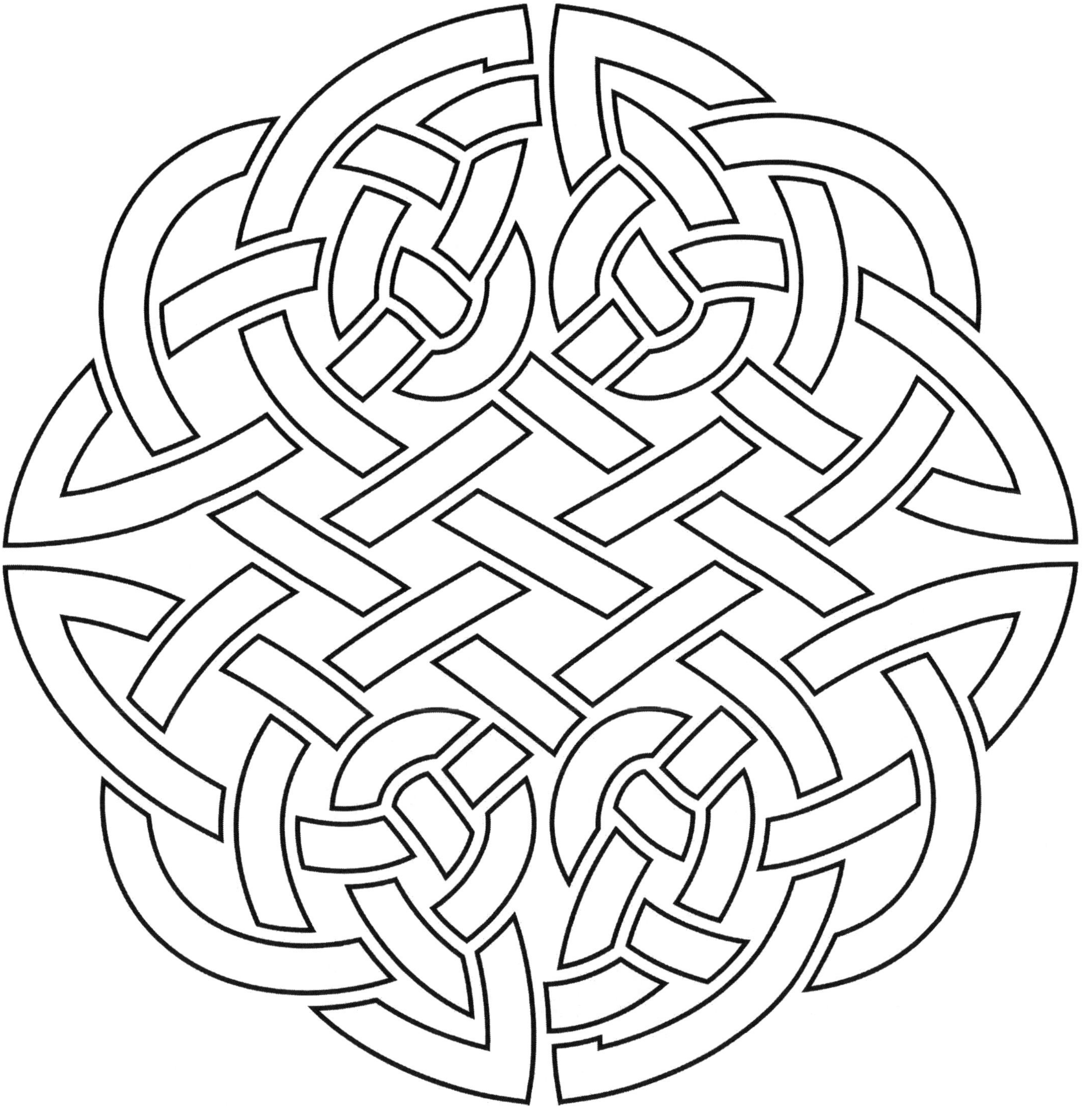

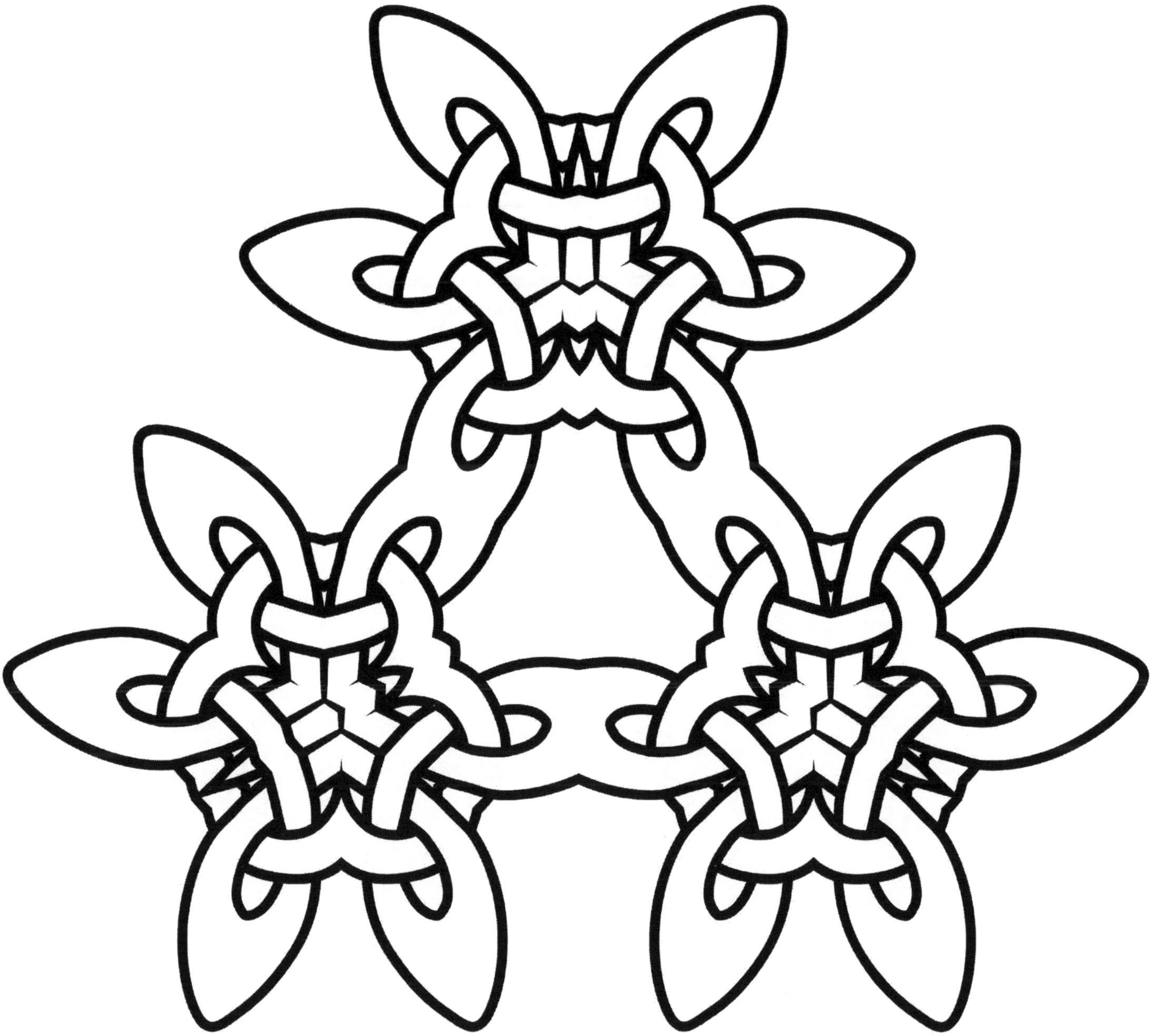

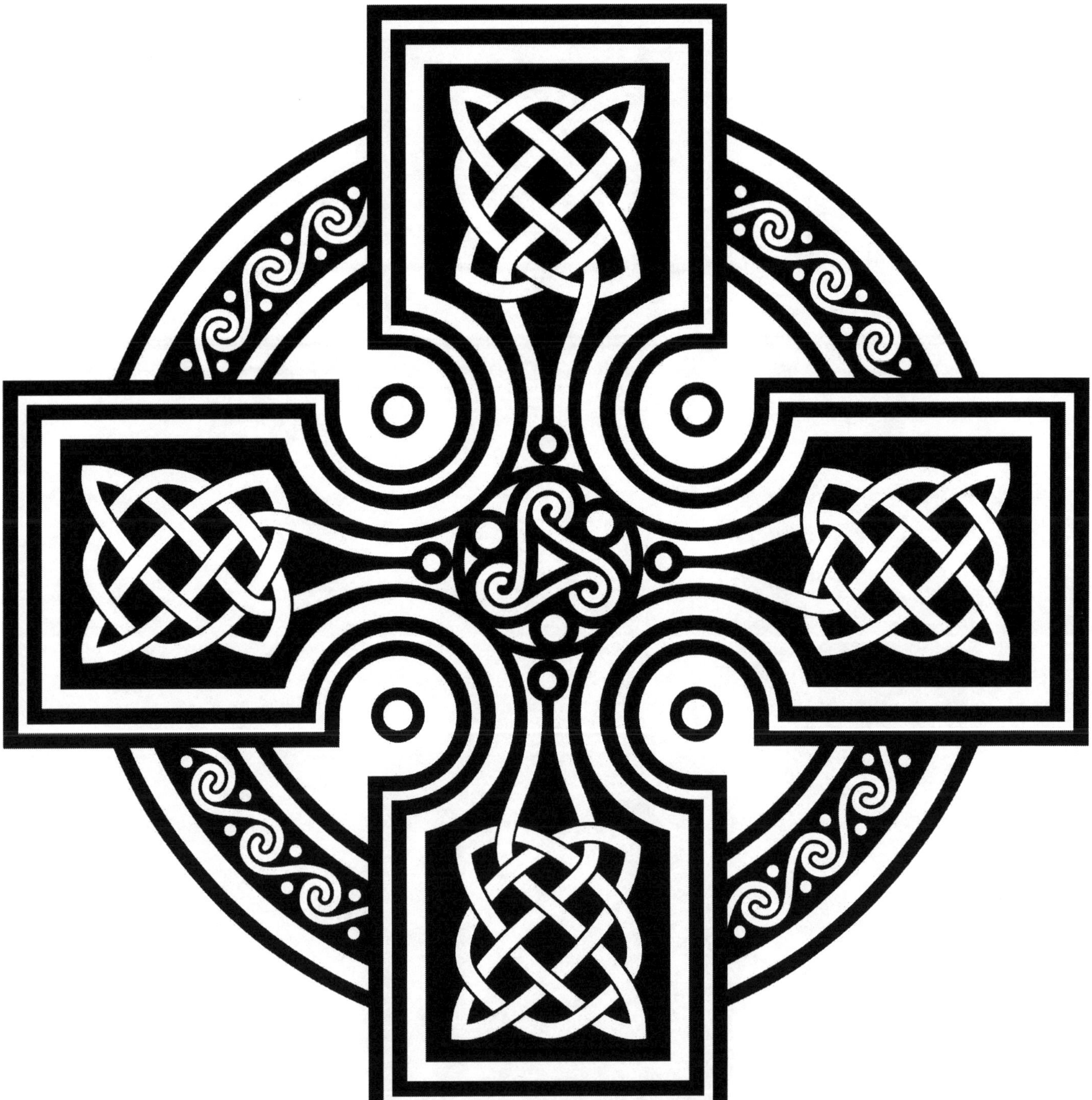

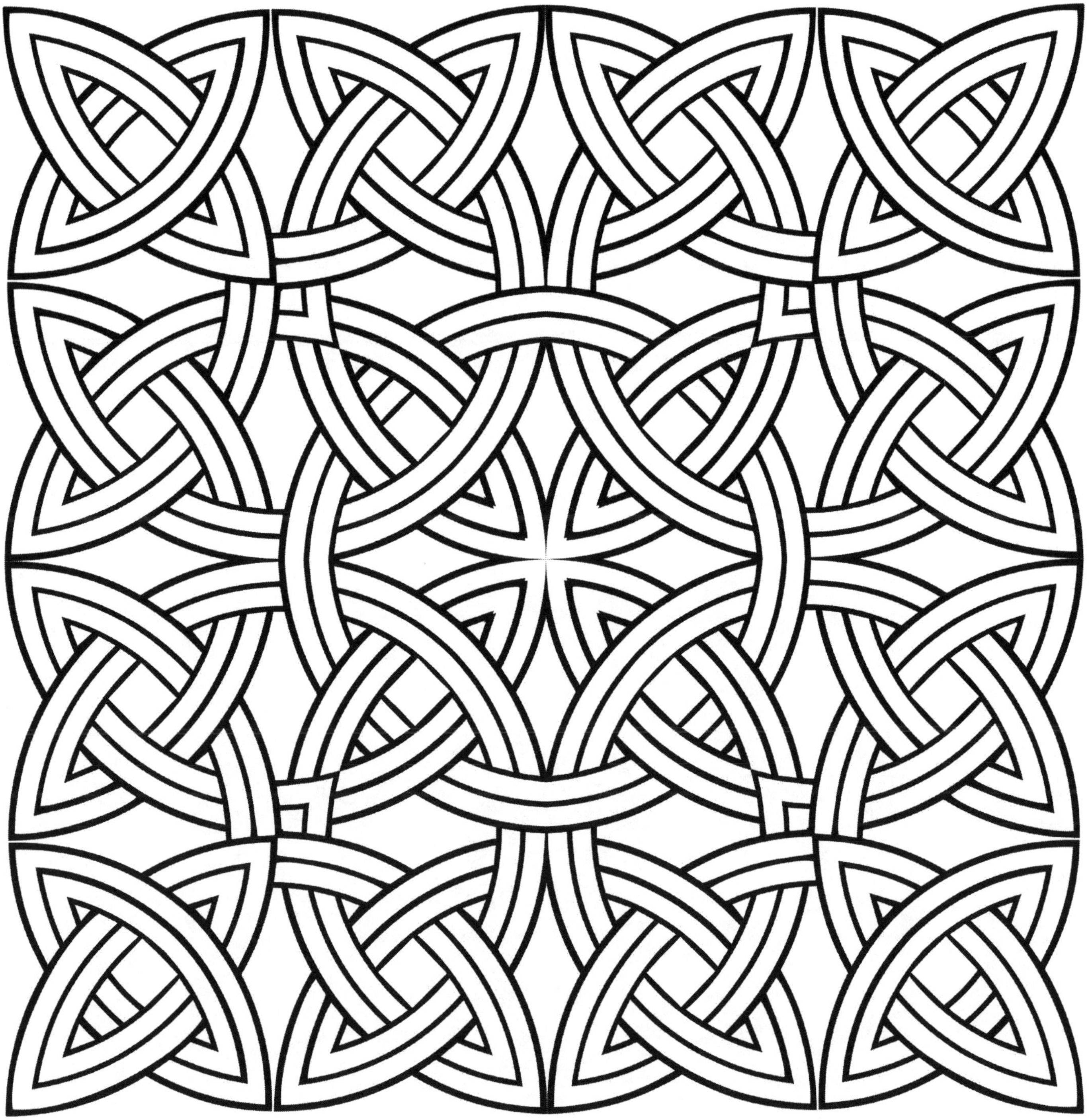

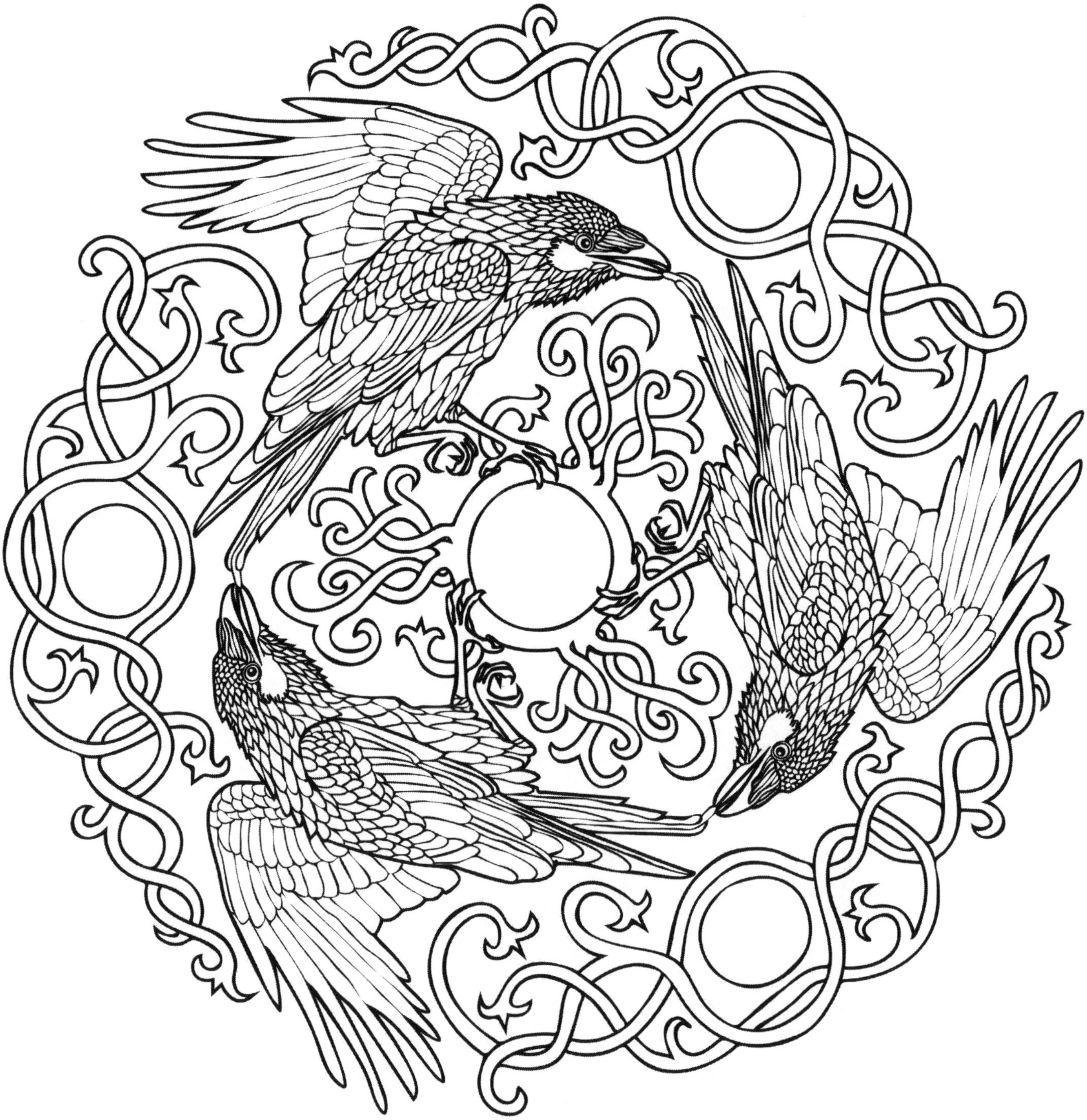

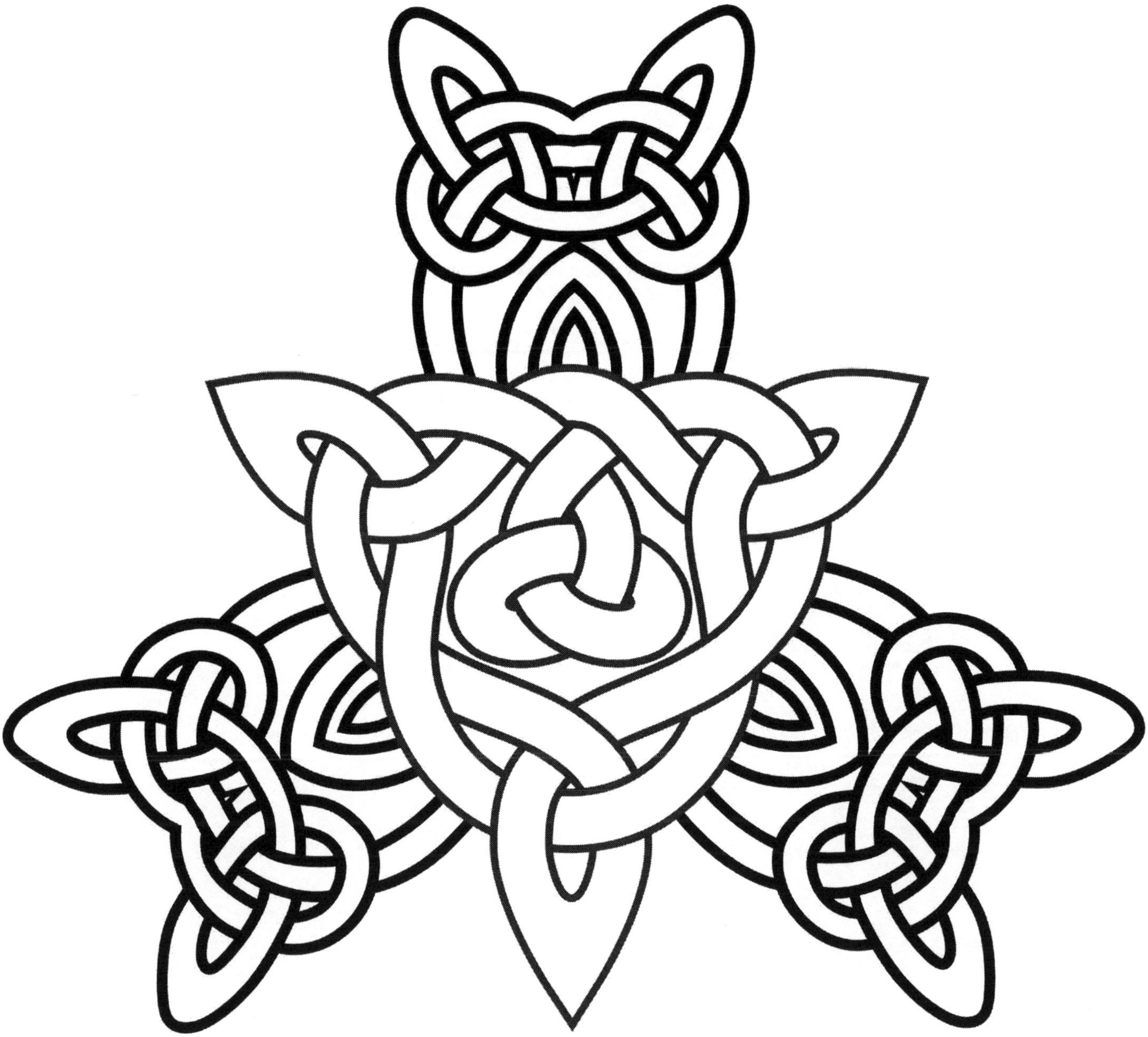

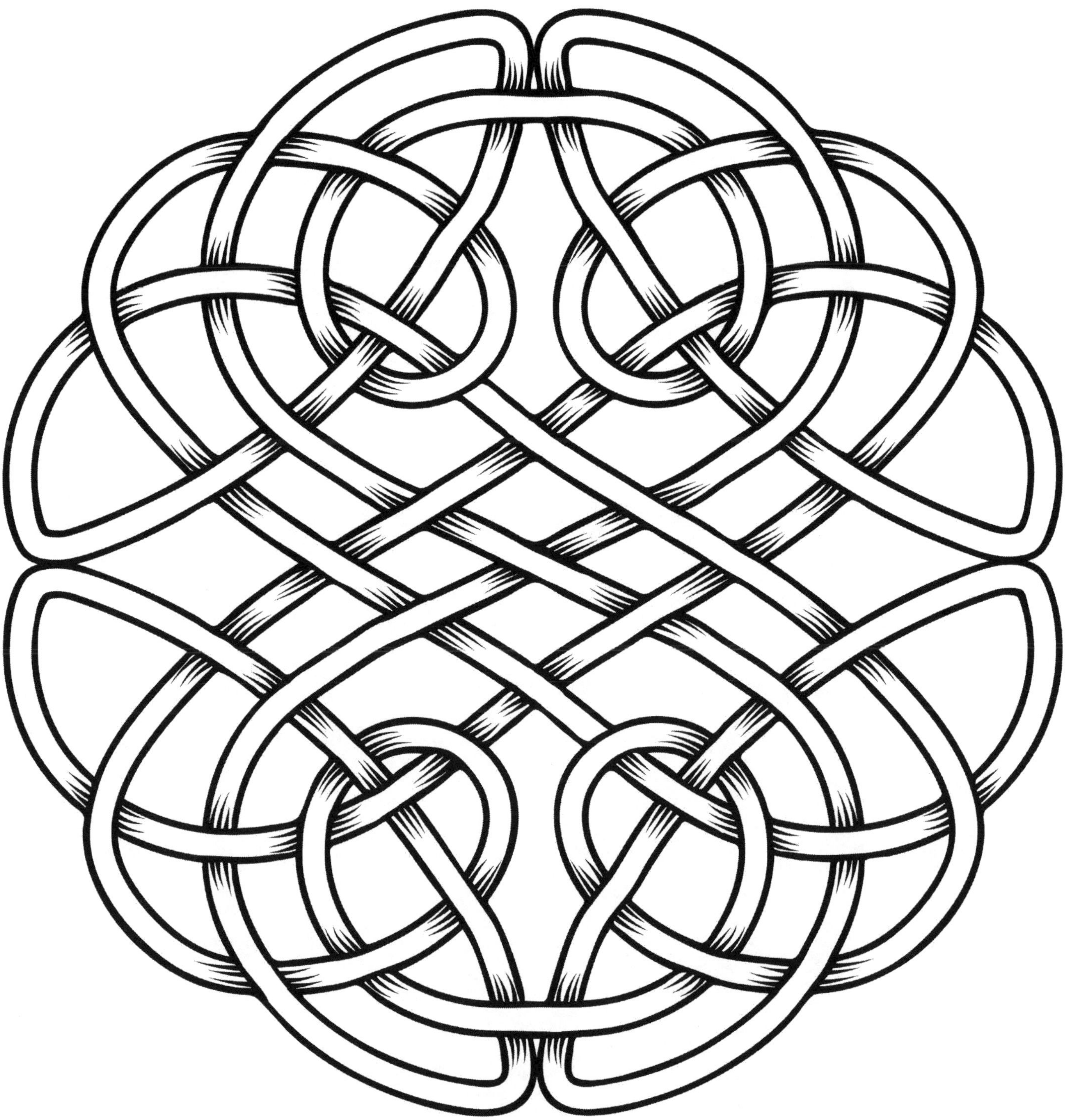

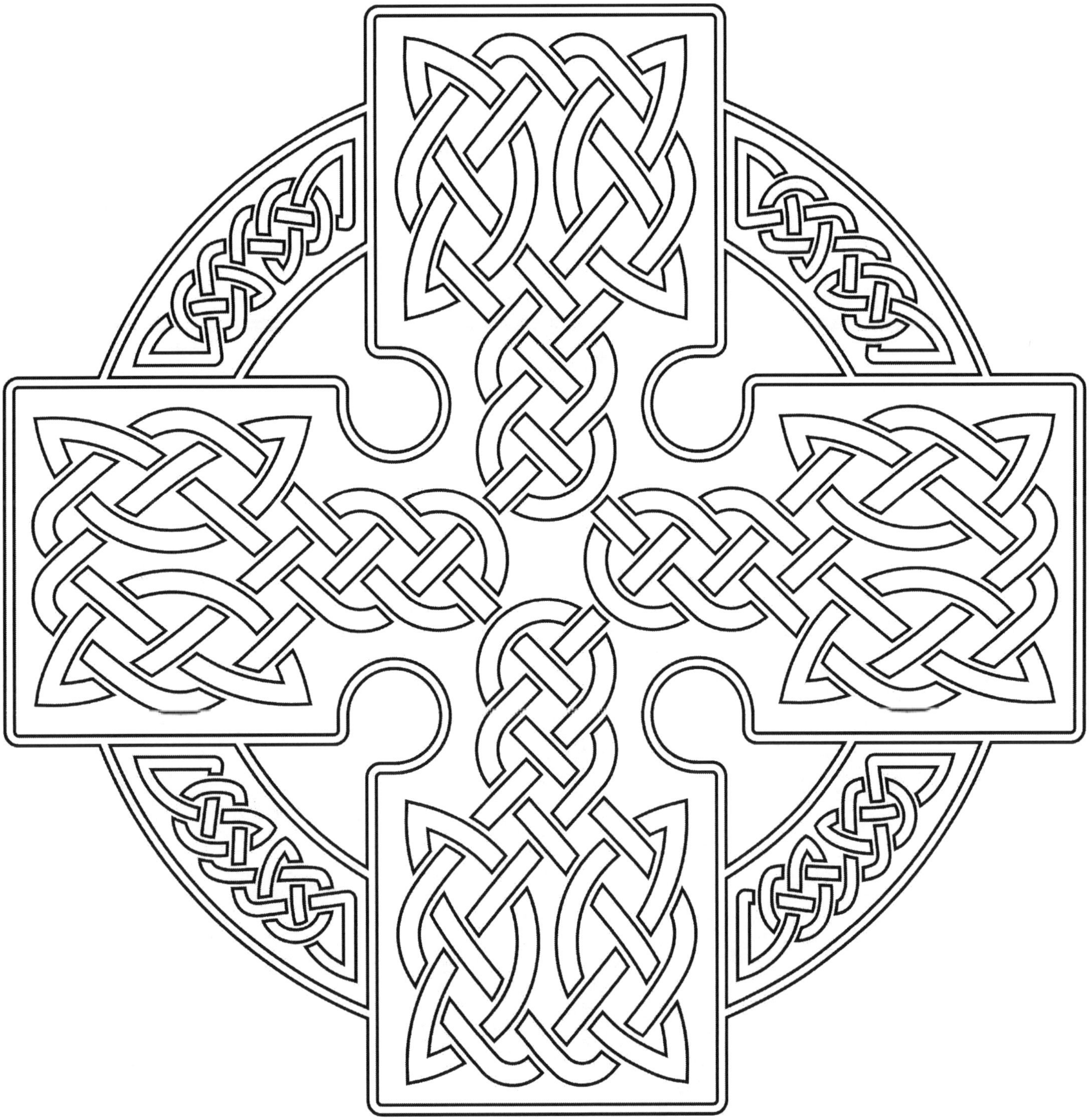

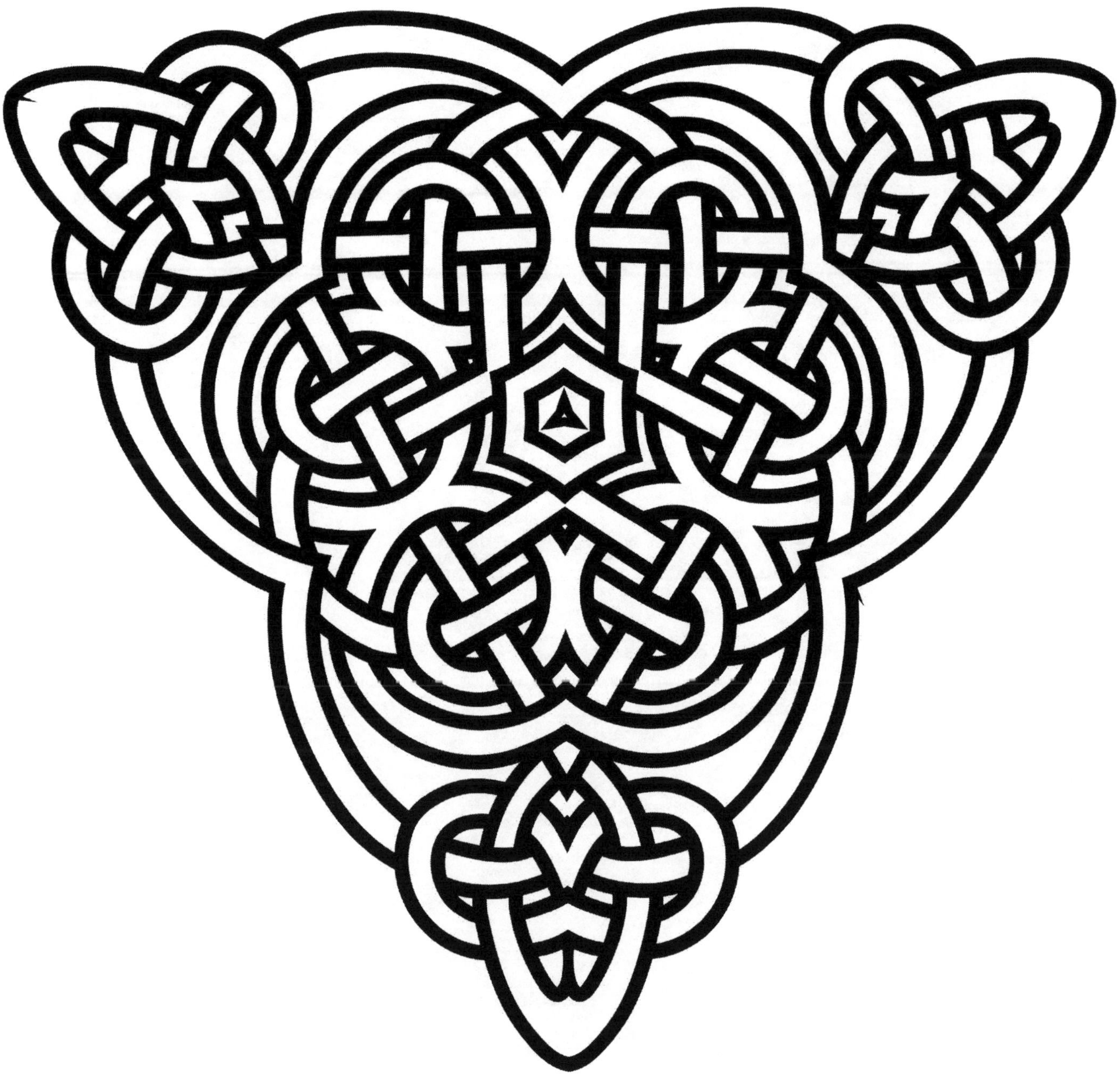

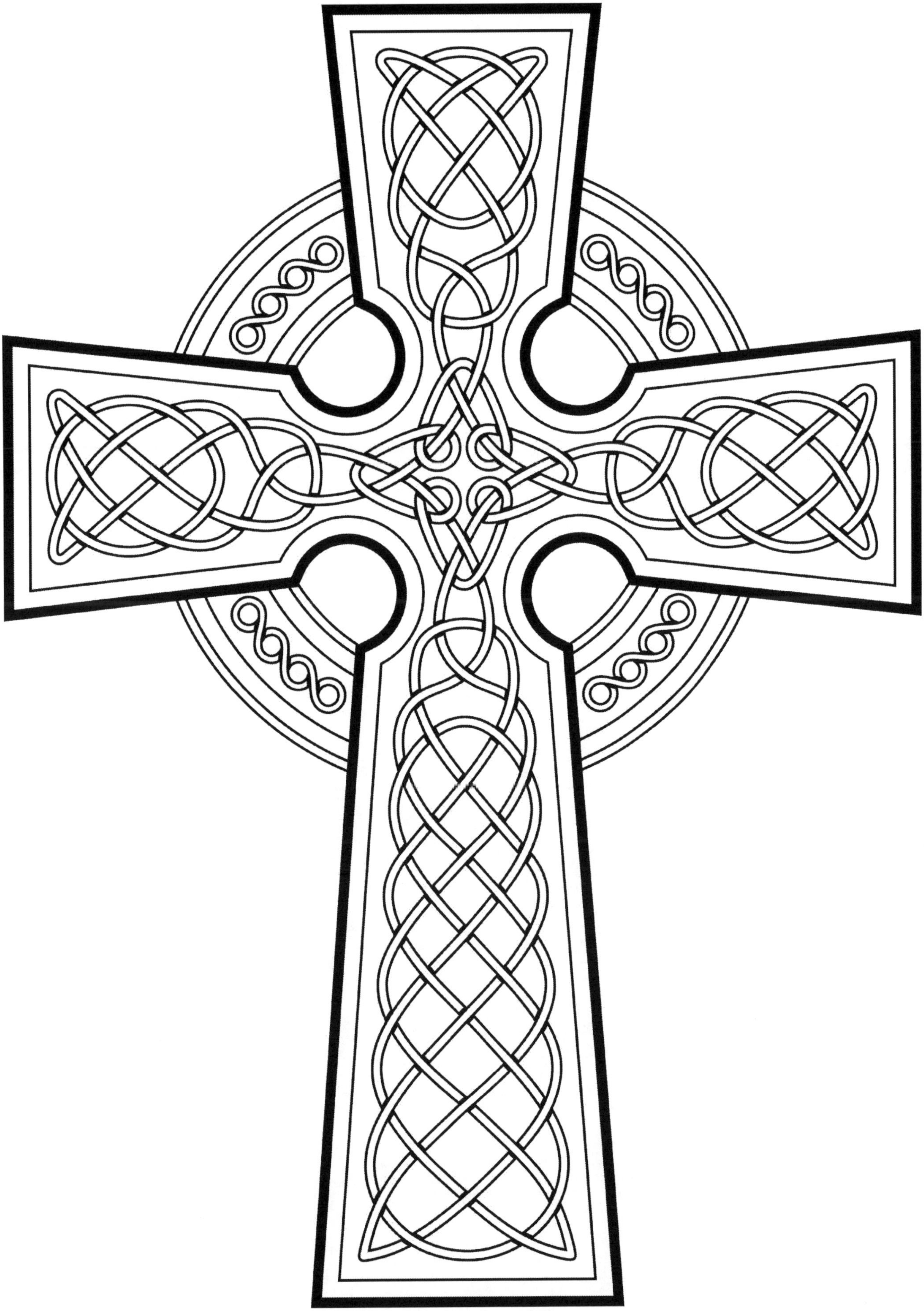

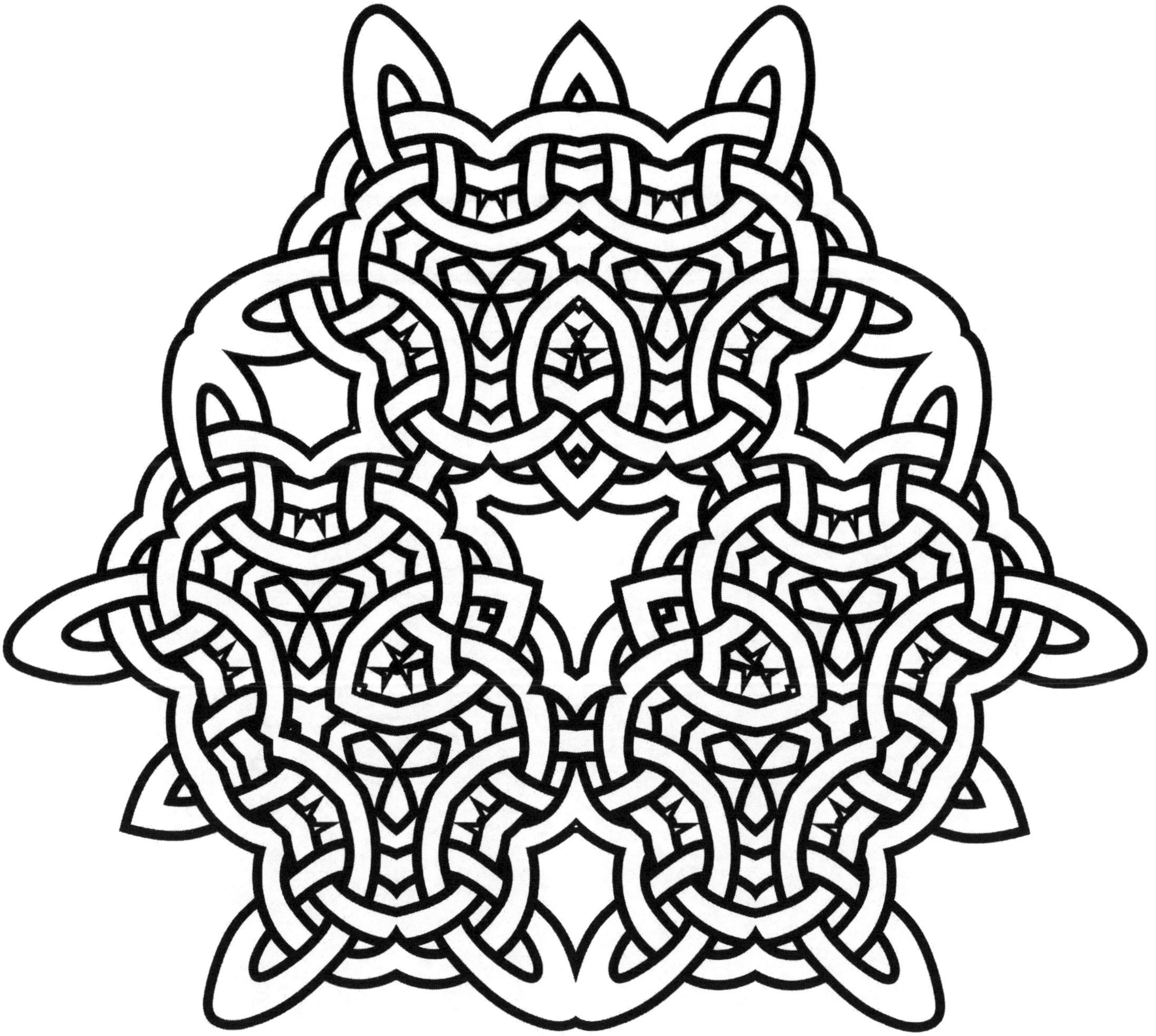

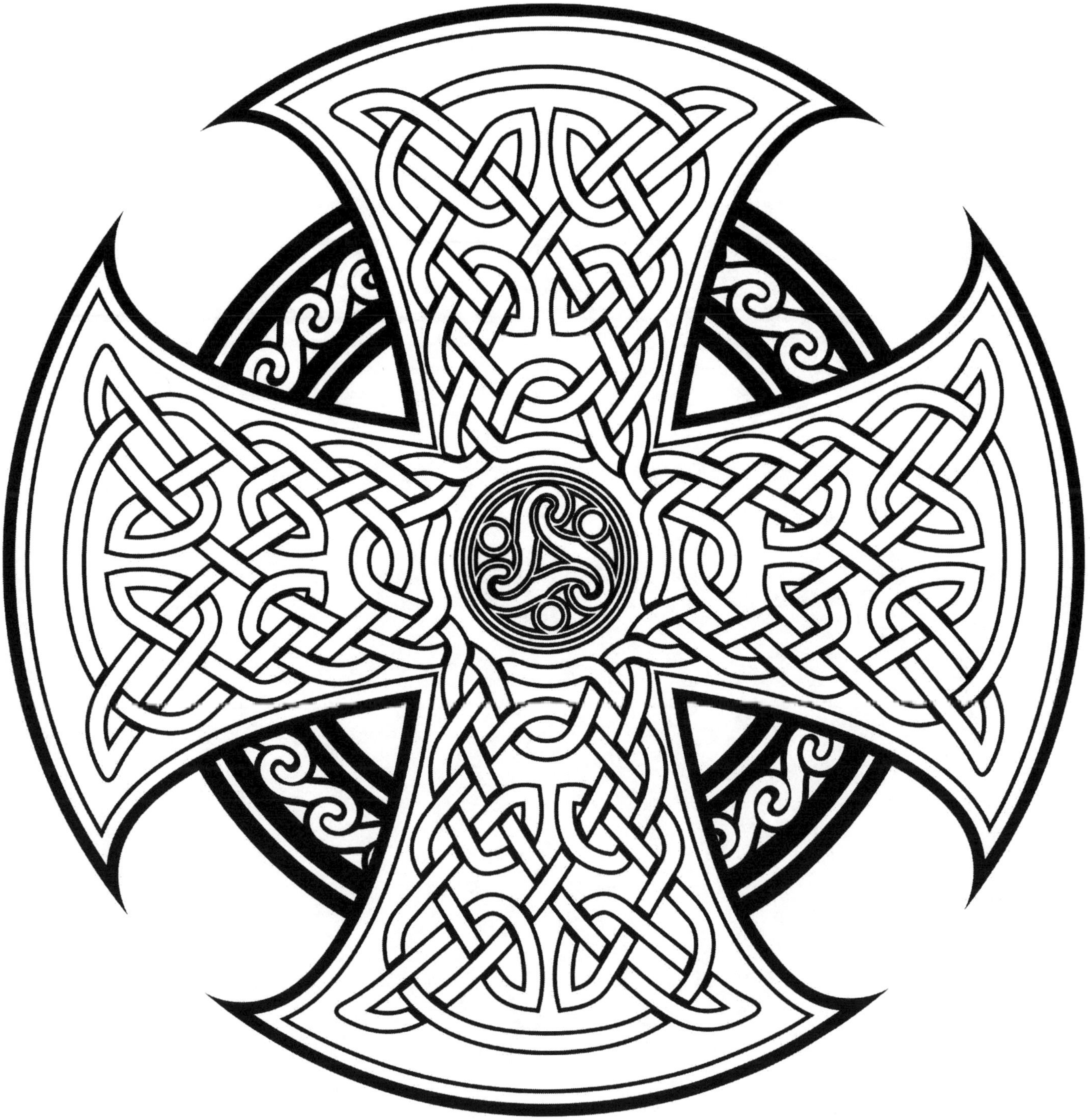

Made in the USA
Monee, IL
04 December 2023

48169956R00057